D0784864

DOCTOR'S ORDERS

John Scally

DOCTOR'S ORDERS?

Towards a New Medical Ethics

VERITAS

Published 2001 by
Veritas Publications
7/8 Lower Abbey Street
Dublin 1

ISBN 1 85390 582 8

British Library Cataloguing
in Publication Data.
A catalogue record for
this book is available
from the British Library.

Cover design by Donny Keane
Printed in the Republic of Ireland by Betaprint Ltd, Dublin

Veritas books are printed on paper made from the wood pulp of
managed forests. For every tree felled, at least one tree is planted,
thereby renewing natural resources.

To the staff of the
Department of Hebrew, Biblical and Theological Studies
in Trinity College, Dublin,
who generously sponsored the research for this book
through their Elrington Research Fellowship
and
to the members of 'Parents for Justice'.

CONTENTS

ACKNOWLEDGEMENTS

This book was made possible by the assistance of the Department of Hebrew, Biblical and Theological Studies in Trinity College, Dublin, through their Elrington Research Fellowship.

I am particularly grateful to Dr Maureen Junker-Kenny and Professor Seán Freyne for their interest in my research.

I would like to express my thanks to Breda Butler, Pat and Josephine Cleere, Jackie Gallagher of the Irish Haemophilia Society, Dr Deirdre Madden, Margaret McKeever, Fionnuala O'Reilly, Annie Ryan, Proinsias de Rossa, Bernard Smullen and Charlotte Yates.

I wish to express my gratitude for the ongoing friendship of Linda Golden.

I am deeply grateful to Professor Bill Shannon and Professor Werner Jeanrond for encouraging my interest in medical ethics.

I am grateful to Raphael Gallagher who inspired my interest in medical ethics because of his wonderful humanity and his great teaching skills.

My gratitude to my good friend Tony Draper for his help and encouragement in recent years.

I am indebted to Maura Hyland, Toner Quinn and all at Veritas for their help and encouragement.

INTRODUCTION

First it was the Church, then, in quick succession, politics, business, the banks, the judges. Now it seems it is the turn of the medical profession to have its reputation tarnished.

The inherent trust that is an essential element in the relationship between doctors and their patients has been threatened by recent controversies – notably the revelation that Irish hospitals were harvesting the organs of dead children without the consent of their parents and that many people acquired hepatitis C or HIV from contaminated blood. Who will ever forget the distressing details of the Brigid McCole case?

Of course, this is not just an Irish phenomenon. Last year at Sheffield's Northern General hospital, more than 150 expectant mothers anxiously awaited the birth of their babies after a computer error over their Down's Syndrome tests. If such a calamity was an isolated one, it would be a matter of concern. But it was not. It almost pales into insignificance when compared with the scandal of its botched paediatric cardiac surgery. The Ritchie inquiry produced a damning indictment on a consultant gynaecologist, Rodney Ledward, who ruined the lives of scores of women. His contempt for his patients, who put their welfare in his hands, continued for over ten years before he was suspended. Even more alarming was that his conduct went unchallenged by his peers for so long – highlighting the inadequacies of the profession's system of surveillance and investigation.

While the failures in the system are very disquieting, it is for most people the one-to-one interaction between patients and doctors that gives serious ground for concern. Sir Donald Irvine, president of the General Medical Council, with commendable honesty observed, 'some doctors still think they're playing God'. He went on to relate a recent incident between a consultant and the distressed relative of a patient who wanted to know why she had suffered complications. The consultant's words: 'I shouldn't have to answer these questions. I don't normally talk to patients or the relatives about these matters'.

In George Eliot's *Middlemarch,* Dr Casaubon responds to the hope and ardour of his young wife Dorothea with a timid, passive-aggressive attitude, 'I'm not listening to you, and anyway I know better'. Casaubon is threatened by Dorothea's energy and idealism and by the thought of change. Today the medical profession sometimes appears to share Dr Casaubon's mindset, as is apparent in the recent storm of controversies in Ireland.

Many people are frantically waiting for admission to hospitals. When they finally get a bed, however, they do not expect to be ignored or have their trust betrayed. An anthropologist would probably consider the debate over the doctor's power over a patient as a classic case of the 'top dog' and 'underdog', with the top dog firmly clinging to its privileged position.

One of the characters in Tom Stoppard's play *Professional Foul* incisively remarks, 'There would be no moral dilemmas if moral principles worked in straight lines and never crossed each other.' The harsh reality is that in all aspects of life, health care included, moral principles do cross each other.

Human life is problematic, insofar as life proceeds by decisions, which we take at a particular time. To become human involves more than merely reacting to stimuli; we are moulded by the fundamental values, principles and rules that take on a life form when we act in freedom, that is, when we act in a particular way and give our personal allegiance to that choice. It is because we can shape our lives that questions arise about how we should do so.

The capacity for shaping our life by choice and freedom is central to our development. It is also at the core of ethical decision-making. In many cases ethical choices do not occur in conditions where right and wrong are apparent, but rather the best decision must be wrenched from less than ideal alternatives. In no field of human activity is this more apparent than in the practice of medicine. For this reason medical ethics is not an optional extra but a constituent part of the practice of medicine.

In this book we will read some powerful testimonies of people with unhappy experiences of the medical profession and the Irish health-care system. However, this is not an exercise in naming and shaming or a cheap exercise in sensationalism. These testimonies highlight the fact that when we are talking about medical ethics we are not talking about some abstract concept: we are talking about real flesh and blood people with real flesh and blood problems. Although we will be examining, for example, stories of parents whose children's organs were harvested without their consent, their cases raise issues about medical practice that go way beyond organ retention.

To paraphrase Bob Dylan, the medical times are a changing. In Ireland there appears to be a shift from a social to an economic view of medicine. There is an increasing dichotomy between the super-specialists and the primary health-care providers. Medicine has changed and continues to change rapidly. Society has undergone profound changes. Yet the value system that underlines medical ethics essentially dates back over two thousand years. Is this a satisfactory situation? The testimonies we will examine would suggest not. My task in this book is to try to map some lighthouses along the route that the medical profession must navigate in the third millennium.

1

SUFFER NOT THE LITTLE CHILDREN

Death always sends a chill through the bones. Each death is a painful reminder of the ultimate and unwelcome end for us all. It is all the more harrowing when a young child dies and all the promise of a young life is denied. It is possibly for that reason that the recent controversies about the harvesting of children's organs in Irish hospitals touched so many raw nerves. A number of issues quickly came to the surface – the adequacy, or lack of, post-mortem consent; the circumstances of organ and tissue retention at post-mortem and the subsequent disposition of such tissues and organs.

The Department of Health ordered an inquiry to investigate the chain of events and expanded it to examine the links between the hospitals and pharmaceutical companies that may have sought to purchase retained organs. This followed the revelation that a Dublin hospital had supplied pituitary glands taken from deceased children to a pharmaceutical company for research on a growth-promotion product in the 1980s. The pituitary glands were taken from the base of the brains of dead children during post-mortem examinations and passed on to the pharmaceutical company once they had been examined by medical specialists. The company is said to have made contributions to the hospital's research fund.

This was not just an Irish phenomenon. While families were always asked for permission to perform autopsies and while the issue of the donation of organs might have been mentioned at that time, in some cases they may not have been explicitly asked to give their consent. Last September the British Health Minister, Susan Deacon, announced an independent review group to investigate the removal and storage of organs without parental permission. An investigation at Bristol University Hospital into the alleged incompetence of a cardiac surgeon led to the revelation that the retention of organs was common practice among pathologists in the UK.

A case in point was that of Liverpool's Alder Hey, where it emerged that they had secretly stored hundreds of organs removed from children's bodies without their parents' consent. One of the men central to this story was the Dutch doctor Professor Dick van Velzen, who left Alder Hey in 1995. In September 2000 Canadian investigators issued an arrest warrant for van Velzen after finding organs from one to two children aged about five in a 12ft by 12ft crate being used to store his personal effects in a garage near the hospital in Dartmouth, Nova Scotia, in Canada, where he worked after leaving the Liverpool hospital. In 1998 he left Canada abruptly after allegations that his post-mortems were not up to standard.

Lorraine
The Bristol case in particular inspired one woman to investigate whether or not similar practices existed in Ireland. The first story in Ireland of organ retention to come into the public arena was that of Lorraine Yates. Her mother, Charlotte, was shocked to open a Sunday newspaper and read the details of Lorraine's life and death. To this day she does not know who leaked the story.

> Lorraine was my second pregnancy. I had one little girl at the time who was three and a half. All the way through the pregnancy I felt there was something wrong but I didn't know what it was. Eventually she arrived and everything was fine. She was very small. She was only 6lb 5oz. I had to take her back every two weeks or so to have her weighed and checked but nobody picked up on anything wrong.
>
> After about seven weeks I went for my own check-up. My father was going to mind Lorraine for me and I was down in my mother's house and I went to give her a bottle before I left. She was limp in the pram and at first we thought she was dead. So my father bundled her into the car and he took her into the hospital. She was fine again by that stage. We waited for five hours for someone to see her and they told us then that she probably had pneumonia. I came home kind of relieved it was just that.

At about eight o'clock that night I rang to see if Lorraine had taken her bottle and I was asked by one of the nurses if Lorraine was baptised and I said no. So they called in a priest from the local church and he baptised her. They told me then that when they did the X-rays on her they found that her heart was in the wrong position in her body and that they were getting a cardiologist from another hospital to look at her and as soon as he came in he started giving a list of instructions that needed to be done. I knew immediately that he was a brilliant doctor and I knew straight away Lorraine could not be in better hands and I would have trusted him with my life. She did have pneumonia and she was transferred to another hospital a week later with a police escort because they reckoned if they didn't get her to a hospital with more sophisticated technology she would die. That was 12 December 1979.

She was there until the following April, Good Friday. She had open heart surgery in March. It emerged she had a condition that meant that the heart wasn't properly formed: the left ventricle hadn't formed; there were two holes in the heart and there was no pumping chamber to pump the blood around.

Her colouring was bad and her breathing was bad. Even when she came home she was backwards and forwards to the hospital. Like any cardiac patient she was very susceptible to chest infections. She had more corrective surgery when she was two and a half and afterwards she was all right although her colouring was bad and she couldn't run like her friends. We minded her well and we gave her a lot of medication.

Eventually the doctor said she could go to school and that nearly broke my heart because I didn't want to leave her and I was worried she mightn't be looked after properly. When you have a sick child you don't trust anybody one hundred per cent to look after them and we had to fight all the way to get her looked after properly.

It was an uphill struggle for Lorraine, for every day of her life. We know we wouldn't have had her for five and a half years of life without the wonderful medical team she had in the hospital. They were absolutely brilliant – when Lorraine was alive.

On 18 June 1985 it was near the last day in Lorraine's first year in school and it was the Sports Day. Lorraine was there just to watch her friends running around and she really enjoyed it. When the Sports Day was over they were all going back to class but Lorraine got very upset and asked that she be brought home and I agreed to that. On our way out we went over to her sister's classroom. Nicky was nine at the time and she opened the window when she saw us. Lorraine said to her, 'I just wanted to tell you that I love you.' They gave each other a kiss.

We were nearly home and I was carrying her because she couldn't walk very far. I put her down so that she could walk a little bit and then she walked on after me. Then I heard her calling, 'Oh, Mammy', and after that she just collapsed. I ran to her but she actually did hit the ground before I got to her. That was my big fear at the time, that she had hit her head and was going to have a bump, but really the problem was that she had a heart attack. It took me a few seconds to realise that.

When I got her to the hospital she was put in intensive care and on a ventilator. I thought, in my innocence, people couldn't die when they were on a ventilator. They didn't know if there was brain damage, so we sat there, and about 9.30 that night something went wrong and the machines started bleeping so we were ushered out of intensive care. They told us later that she had a second heart-attack. Lorraine died at 10.30. She never regained consciousness from the first attack.

I couldn't remember how long it was until I checked the charts but twenty-five minutes after she died they asked about the post-mortem. It was much too soon. We were still too stunned. I remember saying, 'No. You're not doing a post-mortem. She's been through enough', but they said, 'This is a legal thing and you have to do it. It's a coroner's post-mortem.' I was very upset about that. We had to leave at 12.30 or one o'clock. We were told the post-mortem would be early in the morning but the body wouldn't be available until lunchtime.

It was an awful time for us. We got a letter a few months later and it just said the post-mortem confirmed what the doctors thought all along about Lorraine's death.

I got pregnant again and I was terrified that the same thing would happen. I contacted the cardiologist who had dealt with Lorraine and we met and chatted about it and he said to get someone to ring him as soon as the child was born. I had another baby girl and we rang him and he came and checked her and thankfully everything was fine.

In February of 1999 I was sitting at home watching the news when I saw the report about the Royal Infirmary Hospital in Bristol and how organs were harvested from dead children without the consent of their parents. My immediate thought was: could this have happened to Lorraine? I rang the hospital the following day but I was fobbed off for nine weeks, until I eventually got an appointment with the relevant person. The conversation went as follows:

'Did I bury Lorraine without her heart?'

'Yes. You did.'

'What else?'

'Oh, we took her lungs as well, Charlotte.'

'Where are her organs?'

'They were cremated.'

'Cremated? You mean you had a religious service with a priest and everything.'

'Oh, no. Well I suppose I mean incineration.'

'Do you mean to tell me that my child's organs went out with the hospital waste?'

'Yes. I do.'

I can't begin to say how that made me feel. This was my princess – that we had worked so hard to keep alive. We had fought such a battle to keep her alive.

In January 2000 I went with some other members of the Parents for Justice Committee and we had a meeting with some of the relevant personnel in the hospital. They brought us down a corridor and it was only then that I discovered that the mortuary chapel is attached to the laboratory and where they do the post-mortems. We stood in the room the day of her funeral and her heart and her lungs and I don't know what else were next door. Now, that was very, very difficult. I lost a lot of sleep over that.

We knew that they were doing the post-mortem. I did see that Lorraine's scar was still open a tiny bit but she was just after having major surgery. I did see packing and there was kind of cotton wool but the day of the funeral you wouldn't take it in and at this stage I had complete trust in the medical staff and never suspected anything like what happened.

On another occasion we insisted on seeing the pathology laboratory after having endured great resistance initially to that request. To me a laboratory is nice and clean like what you'd see on the television. They brought us to this filthy dirty shed – really two little sheds attached. It was like where you'd put your lawn-mower in. That's where our children's organs were put in. Four of us are running a helpline for people in this situation. We've got thousands of calls. There were 1700 children that we know of in Dublin alone in this situation. Who is responsible for all of this?

We then discovered that it wasn't just children's organs that were harvested. My father died twelve years ago in a different hospital but I've just discovered recently that his brain was taken. He had cancer and as far as I know that's the only organ they took or would have been of any use to them. Conveniently his records have been lost.

It seems very strange to me that your child is the most precious thing in your life and that there are medical people telling you what you can and can't know about her. They don't seem to understand that although Lorraine is dead I, and people like me in similar situations, need answers. It's so sad.

A Miracle Baby

Fionnuala O'Reilly's son, Michael, died after just twenty-three weeks of life. Five years later she discovered that Michael's heart and lungs had been retained without her consent.

At twenty weeks into my pregnancy I knew that Michael had a defect that was incompatible with life. The hospital prepared me for that. From the beginning I requested information irrespective of how painful that information was going to be. I felt that was my right and that nobody had the right to make a judgement on whether I was prepared or able to absorb that information, only myself. That right was respected by the hospital up until the point of my child's death.

Michael was born on 20 July 1994. He was my miracle baby because he was only expected to live an hour, maybe an hour and a half. In fact, all expectations were that he probably would be stillborn. Michael defied all expectations and he lived until he was nearly six months. Within hours of his birth he was transferred to another hospital. I have to say that it was their skill and care that gave me twenty-three weeks with my child and I'll be grateful for that to my dying day and also for the care and compassion they showed me during Michael's life. From his birth Michael had a series of crises and we were on a rollercoaster of hope and despair and the death of this child was always expected.

In mid December 1994 he seemed to be unwell but not serious enough to be rushed into casualty so we brought him into our GP and she noted that there was an abdominal problem and as he was a very compromised little baby with his heart it was always better to err on the side of caution. She said have him checked out in the hospital and that's what we did. We were so delighted because we were told that he had constipation. To be told that your child has such a mundane problem and can be cured with something that you can buy over the counter was wonderful. We went home walking on air from that hospital.

Michael became ill the following Monday and we knew that this time it was more serious. Having said that, the surgeon told us that he was in better condition than he ever had been in his short life and therefore because of this some exploratory surgery would be undertaken. Our consent was sought and willingly given for the surgery to go ahead and Michael was taken into theatre on Tuesday, 13 December 1994. So routine was his surgery deemed that he was scheduled as the last one that day and that was very comforting to us. We kissed Michael goodbye but a little later as I was ringing my sister I heard my name being called over the PA system to return immediately to the ward. In my foolishness I thought that the surgery had gone better than I expected and that Michael was out.

I raced up the stairs but when I got to the ward I knew that things had not gone to plan because a ward sister and the hospital chaplain were approaching me and I asked, 'Is he gone?' They replied, 'No, but it's looking very bad.' His heart arrested three times in surgery. They didn't know the cause of that but his blood pressure was soaring. Even if he did recover there had been no oxygen going to his brain for significant minutes and the prognosis was very bad and to prepare myself for the worst. The medical staff was in tears and I was very moved by their humanity and compassion and still am to this day. Shortly afterwards two senior staff came out to me and shook their heads and they didn't have to say anything. I knew Michael had died.

Finally we managed to track down my husband, Bernard, who had taken my other two children to McDonalds. By this time Michael was dressed and released to me and I was holding him as I had asked to do. He was still warm. They told me that the hearing is the last thing to go so I should thank him and I said all the things I ever wanted to him.

Then Bernard arrived with our two children. The only message he had got was to go to the hospital and he hadn't known to expect anything bad. Margaret was nine and Tony was a week short of his third birthday. Bernard came in and said, 'Oh, he's back', and went over to stroke his head. I said, 'Bernard, he's gone.' He responded, 'Where's he gone? Don't be silly', and he was talking away to him. The surgical and medical staff looked so embarrassed for him. I had to say, 'Bernard, he's dead.' My husband is a very dark-skinned man and I literally saw the blood drain from his face and I really thought he was going to collapse. My daughter started screaming hysterically like you'd see in a film. The staff were very kind to the children.

Time slows down to a crawl and that's why I very clearly remember what happened next. The surgical registrar left the room and came back and he said that as Michael had died within twenty-four hours of admission to the hospital, that a post-mortem would be ordered by the Dublin city coroner and that I was being told out of courtesy and that my consent was not an issue. I even asked if I had anything to sign. I asked what would a post-mortem involve. I was told that it would entail a short little look as to what had gone on. I was glad that such rigour would be gone into to establish what caused a child's death. Michael was brought down into the mortuary and put into the most beautiful Moses basket and in the most child-friendly environment, with plenty of toys.

When I was informed that the coroner had ordered a post-mortem I even asked would any of Michael's organs be of use to anybody seeing he had died so unexpectedly, so the opening was there for them to tell me that post-mortem involved the retention of some organs for whatever reason, but they told me that his organs were too diseased. They even thanked me for the thought.

The following day I returned after the post-mortem. When I went in they asked me if I would like to dress Michael. I was accompanied by a staff nurse who told me that there was going to be incisions, stitches and that there was going to be a lot of bandaging. I was prepared, but I wasn't prepared for the size of the incisions by any means. There was a huge incision from the bottom of his neck, down his chest and down his abdomen. There was a further incision under his left arm, and to this day the incision that puzzled me the most was the one that was down his back. I was aghast. Time slows to a virtual halt and I clearly remember asking, 'Is my baby intact?'

I knew it wasn't the same baby that I held the previous night. She asked, 'What do you mean?'

'Has he everything?'

'He has all the bits and bobs he was born with.'

These words have stuck with me to this day. I was reassured and I dressed him.

We were told that the results of the post-mortem would be sent on to our GP, but that never happened. They told us that we'd be called into the hospital after six weeks. The hospital didn't get in touch with us, so about five months later we went in to discuss the case. We were told that it appeared that when the surgeon touched the bottom of Michael's large intestine that cardiac arrest had occurred. It would appear that the intestine had been rotting.

It wasn't until September 1999 when I read Charlotte Yates's story in the newspaper that the story developed. I just knew that something similar had happened to my child. I rang the hospital after a lot of agonising and within an hour a consultant pathologist had got back to me and explained to me why organ retention was necessary on a post-mortem.

On 17 November I had a meeting with a senior staff member in the hospital. I don't think I've ever met a more arrogant or indifferent individual in my life. It was a combination of this man's approach to this very sensitive issue, his patronising attitude to myself, as well as my horror at what I heard in that interview that expedited the formation of Parents for Justice.

He sat on a table swinging his legs and repeatedly looked at his watch and his bleeper. I got a big, long lecture about post-mortems. Then I asked him about Michael and he looked at his file. He remarked that it was very interesting and asked me if I had known that Michael had virtually no pancreas. I said I didn't know that.

He was constantly using a lot of medical jargon. I repeatedly asked him to make this accessible to me because this was important. He did his best. There was a social worker there and he was better.

The senior man said then, 'Michael's heart and lungs were retained, but good news, they were retained in the hospital.' I was told that Michael's heart and lungs were somewhere in a bucket of formalin. I was expected to find great comfort in this but I was outraged. I asked why my consent wasn't sought but he told me that it would have been too distressing to approach a family at a time of death. That's a judgement other people are not qualified to make. There's nothing more distressing than being told your child is dead.

Michael's heart would have been an interesting 'specimen' because the left side was totally underdeveloped. There was half a heart there. He kept referring to Michael's heart and lungs as 'units' and as part of a 'batch'. I asked could I see them but I was told no. With every word he spoke, my anger was rising. The man kept looking at his bleeper in increasing desperation. I said, 'You better stop looking at that bleeper because if it goes off I am going to follow you and shout out my questions in public.' He took me at my word. After more probing he told me I wouldn't have understood five years ago. There are no words to describe his paternalism.

I have no doubt he looked at my address, which was at Inchicore, Dublin 8, at that time, and I'm certain in my mind that he was making value judgements and that he was surprised that somebody articulate and reasonably intelligent could correspond with that address, because he asked me if I was still living in Inchicore. I told him I was living in Carlow now.

We contacted the hospital again three weeks after that. We collected Michael's organs on 13 December 1999, five years to the day after Michael died, and no family should be put in that position.

A measure of how absurd the whole situation is, is that I consider myself lucky to have the privilege of being able to open my child's grave and put in the organs that were retained because so many parents can't do that because they were burnt as hospital waste.

The day we collected Michael's organs we met with the same man again. He was much more humane this time but I was aghast to hear him say on this day of traumatic days in this grotesque situation that what Parents for Justice were doing would set medicine back thirty years. There is a place for that debate, but not on that day. You wouldn't wish it on your worst enemy that they would have to open their child's grave.

I can't tell you how angry I am that a post-mortem was obtained under false pretences. Not only did people omit to give me information, they deliberately lied. I was told that my consent was implied, but there was no way that my consent was implied. I don't know why there were so many evasions and lies. The medical profession in general needs to be much more concerned with their communication skills and to be much less paternalistic.

Sinéad

Margaret McKeever discovered that the heart of her daughter Sinéad was retained without her consent. Her many interactions with a variety of health-care professionals raise important issues about the doctor-patient relationship.

Sinéad was born on 5 April 1977 and she weighed seven pounds, seven ounces, and when I was told I had a little girl I was thrilled because I already had a little boy. At the beginning everything was fine. She was born on a Tuesday and on the Thursday the doctor was examining her because I was going home the next day. I was out of the ward at the time and I can still remember the doctor's face when I came back and he turned and said to me, 'Your baby has a heart murmur.' I didn't realise what that meant and I was too frightened to ask.

He said, 'She's got to go for an X-ray and a cardiograph', and she was brought back to me and I was allowed to go home, but they said, 'We'll check on her every day or two.' I only lived across the road. So I was okay with that.

I took Sinéad home. She was a good baby and I couldn't see anything wrong with her. The following Friday I was back with her. As soon as I walked in, this paediatrician asked me, 'Do you notice anything about your baby's colour?' To me she was just my baby and I didn't notice anything wrong with her. He said,

'She's a greyish-bluish colour.' I was under a bit of stress with a new baby and a little toddler to look after and hadn't noticed anything. He took her off me and said, 'We'll have to admit her. She's very ill.' I remember going up to the ward. She was stripped to her nappy and what I remember is her chest pumping up and down.

From then on it was a nightmare. I tried to feed her and she'd vomit everything up. I was told then they were moving her to a more specialised hospital. I vividly recall being told a lot of medical jargon that I didn't understand at the time and hearing the words, 'Your baby has a congenital heart defect.' I was too embarrassed to ask what that meant. I can remember the doctor from Sinéad's 'new' hospital telling the doctor from her 'old' one, 'The mother should take the baby home. She needs twenty-four hours' care and we don't have the staff to do it.' The old hospital was a little alarmed by this and took her back for a week. From then on it was just hospitals, doctors and a series of infections, really a nightmare.

I brought her back to the first hospital and a doctor took her in the palm of his hand. It looked to me like he was examining a chicken. He said, 'She's perfect in every way but unfortunately she's got a very bad heart.' I dressed my baby and was going for the door when he said, 'By the way, Mrs McKeever, your baby has only six months to live. That'll be her lifespan.' I thought he was going to say something like, 'You forgot her bonnet.'

I was left to walk home alone. I crossed the road in a complete daze. I don't know how I wasn't killed. Then I fell apart. There was nobody to turn to for help.

I wanted Sinéad to have a normal life but it was a 24-hour day minding her – the sickness, infections, worry and sleepless nights. She was very blue. She couldn't walk very far. She had very little energy. It took forever to feed her.

I couldn't explain to my family what it was that was wrong with my child because every time I went to the doctors they used the medical words. They never tried to sit me down and explain what it was that was wrong with Sinéad.

There were always doctors examining her with their class of medical students because she was a very complicated case and the students would ask all kinds of questions about her condition.

That went on until Sinéad was five and we heard that there had been an operation that had been pioneered in England by an Irish man and that it was very complicated, very risky – but without it she only had six months to live. We decided it would be best to go for surgery. She spent eight or nine hours in the theatre. Afterwards the surgeon came out and said, 'She's breathing but that's all. She's patched like a bicycle tube. It's worse than we ever thought it was.' We watched her coming up from the theatre. We could see nothing apart from her chest, which was cut all over. She was covered in machines. They told us that if it worked the blueness would go and she would be pink and that the next twenty-four hours would be crucial but there was nothing we could do and therefore we should go home and get some rest. We were only home an hour when we got a call saying that Sinéad had internal bleeding and they couldn't stop it. They had to take her back to the theatre again and I went mad because how could a five-year-old child survive this – after a nine-hour major operation. I didn't know what it meant at the time for a heart to be put on a by-pass machine.

At 6.30 the following morning the surgeon rang and told us that Sinéad was in trouble again and they had to insert a pacemaker from the outside of her body. She couldn't survive theatre again. She got a relapse the next day. Her lungs collapsed. She had tubes coming from everywhere. They nearly lost her I don't know how many times. The doctors and nurses were excellent and only through them Sinéad survived. She was in intensive care for three and a half weeks. When she finally opened her eyes I went home that night thinking it was great and that she was on the mend. The next day she got a relapse and we were back to the cycle of crises over again.

When she finally recovered her whole features had changed. She went in a chubby, blue girl and came out a slim, pink one. Then the problems came back again and she was having suctions and going on drips. She was five and a half years old and she asked me, 'Am I going to die?' What could I say? I answered, 'Of course you're not going to die.' I came out of the corridor and I cried my eyes out.

We were determined that Sinéad was going to live as normal a life as possible in the circumstances. She went to school but there were a lot of crises on the way.

When she was fourteen one of her cousins in England asked her to be her bridesmaid. I asked the hospital if it would be okay for me to bring her on a plane. She wasn't feeling well at that stage. She was having pains in her chest and pains in her lungs. I told them about this but they assured me that she was okay to travel. I was made to feel that I was an over-protective mother. It had got to the stage where my child could only walk a few yards without having to take a rest. While we were in England Sinéad was very tired all the time. I knew something was wrong. When I got back I took her to the hospital for her July appointment. The doctor informed me that she was bleeding from the heart to the lung and that she needed emergency surgery. I said to him, 'You let me take her to England like that.' I asked when the surgery would be and they said about eight months. I took Sinéad home.

Not too long afterwards she went back into hospital for a catharisation. They wouldn't let me into the theatre with her. She was very upset, and you do this procedure when you're awake. She came out and I offered to wash her but she said, 'No there's blood everywhere.' I said, 'Ah sure it's nothing I've never seen before.' I was totally shocked when I saw all the blood. I didn't know why. They never told me. The next day she was discharged. Before she went out a junior doctor came out and said, 'Sinéad, I've to check you. You haemorrhaged yesterday.' This child I reared could have died with all the haemorrhaging but nobody bothered to tell me.

Some time later I rang up the hospital to see if she could be vaccinated against German measles in school and I was told she couldn't, and by the way her surgery would be in two weeks.

A week before the operation Sinéad was very nervous. We brought her to see a specialist. He was very, very nice to her, but after he checked her out he asked to see me alone. Then he said, 'How am I going to tell you what I have to tell you about that beautiful girl out there? I'm terrified of touching her. I'm terrified. There's so much scarring on the tissue inside that if I touch it she's going to hemorrhage immediately, but she needs this operation.'

I nearly collapsed.

I asked, 'What happens if we don't do it?'

He replied, 'She'll die soon and she'll be walking around with oxygen.'

I knew she could not cope with that.

The surgery was on 23 October 1991. She was very upset. It was like she knew she wasn't coming back. She became hyper and was very panicky. Sinéad went into the theatre at eleven. I can remember the singer Sandy Kelly was there with somebody who had a sick child in the hospital.

After a while the sister brought us into a little storeroom and told us that Sinéad had died. My husband passed out with the shock.

Within a very short time a doctor approached me and asked if I would be willing to donate Sinéad's cornea. The way I was feeling at the time I would have liked somebody to donate a heart to Sinéad if she needed it so I said yes, if it was okay with her father.

They took us down to a day ward where Sinéad was laid out. I couldn't believe she was so cold so quickly. It was because she had haemorrhaged everywhere when they took her off the by-pass machine. I thought I would have a warm child to hold but she was like a marble statue.

After we left Sinéad the same doctor approached me and his exact words were, 'I've been sent to ask you would you allow us to do a post-mortem. The coroner probably wouldn't order it because Sinéad died in the theatre.' I felt I couldn't refuse them. I felt intimidated. My husband signed a form but we had no idea what was on it.

I took three steps away from this doctor and I knew straight away I had made a big mistake. I thought to myself: How could I allow them to cut her up again? What kind of mother was I to let them do that? I had years of having to live with that.

I was never at peace with the decision to donate the cornea. Three times I rung up the hospital to see if they had taken her eyes but three times they said no, 'It's just the film in front of her eyes.' Then I had a letter from the Eye and Ear Hospital thanking me for the gift of her eyes. I rang the sister I knew in the hospital where Sinéad died, in a hysterical state, but again I was told no, it was just the film.

After all that heartbreak I just wanted to die. I co-founded a bereavement group in the hospital so that other people wouldn't feel they were alone.

A few years later I heard on the television about Bristol and never dreamed it would happen in Ireland. I heard about somebody on the news being very upset about a hospital in Dublin and it was something to do with organs. The following day I was reading the editorial in *The Star*. The heading was 'Shame'. I saw that Sinéad's hospital was reported to have retained organs.

I just knew.

I rang up the hospital and finally I got talking to a pathologist. He talked a lot of jargon but didn't answer any of my questions really. We got an appointment to meet a pathologist and a social worker. I will never forget this man. He sat on the table with his legs swinging and his whole attitude was: why are you bothering me and wasting my time? He went on and on with the same jargon about procedures until finally my husband got fed up with it and asked, 'What did ye take?'

He answered, 'We took her heart.'

'What did ye do with it?'

'We incinerated it.'

I said I wanted to speak with Charlotte Yates but they didn't put me in touch with her. I found her myself.

I cried and cried and when I got home I stood under Sinéad's picture and I apologised to her.

I couldn't rest without finding out about my daughter's eyes. I showed the letter to somebody else and he said he would check it out for me. A month later he came back and told me, 'Yes. They took out her eyes.'

There's no words to explain the hurt we feel about all this. We want the health-care professionals who were responsible for this hurt to be fully accountable for their actions. They will never know the hurt they caused.

Heartbreak

Cork woman, Breda Butler, suffered great distress because of the death of her son, Joseph. However, her pain has been compounded by the manner in which she has learned the precise circumstances of his death and the tortuous way the details of what happened to his organs have emerged.

My son, Joseph, was born in Limerick on 27 May 1995. When he was two days old he began to change colour and was feeling unwell. He was transferred to the hospital in Dublin where he was diagnosed as having congenital heart disease, i.e., a transposition of the great arteries with a large hole between two chambers of his heart.

Joseph was let home after three days with medication and he was to go back two weeks later for his catharisation. During these two weeks at home Joseph was doing very well. To look at him you would never think he had a heart condition. He was putting on weight like any normal child would. I breastfed him and he was a pleasant baby to feed. He was a very happy baby.

On 12 June 1995 Joseph went back to hospital for his catharisation, which was the next day. He was in the hospital for the next ten days.

Joseph's heart surgery was planned for 24 July. We were told that if he didn't have surgery he would not see his first birthday. At nine o'clock that morning Joseph was taken down to the theatre. At this stage I asked if I could go in with my son in theatre but I was told no. I think any parent who wants to go in with a child in theatre should be allowed to do it. It was very upsetting. Joseph was a private patient.

My husband and I were in the hospital on a bleeper and we were told that we would be in contact with the ward every hour to get an update on his progress. At 2.30 p.m. we were told we could see our son between 3.30 and 4.00 in intensive care. At 3.40 the bleeper came on. We were told by medical staff that they had run into complications. At 4.22 Joseph died.

I asked to see the main surgeon so that he could explain what went wrong. He did not see us. Another doctor came out and said Joseph had to have a coroner's post-mortem. We were told that Joseph died in theatre, that they could not get his heart going with the by-pass machine.

At 6.30 p.m. Joseph was brought back into a little room in the ward. He was still quite warm. I had him for half an hour at least when I saw blood coming out of his blanket. I could see the horror on the staff's faces when they saw me noticing the blood. If yesterday was today I would have opened the blanket.

Members of the family came up from Limerick expecting that we would be bringing Joseph home but we were told that his post-mortem was at 8.00 a.m. the next day and Joseph would not be released until 2.00 p.m. The following day I asked to see the main surgeon again and said I would refuse to leave the hospital until I saw him. He came from another hospital and immediately said to me, 'Hello Mrs Butler. We've met before.' I replied, 'Excuse me doctor, we never met before.' He told me that the bottom line was that they couldn't get his heart going. I found him to be very cold towards me.

I asked him if there was any organs that Joseph might have been able to donate. He said, 'No, except maybe his eyes.' At that very moment they were doing an autopsy and removing his organs.

I brought home my son in my own arms to Cork. In the car I just talked to him as if he was asleep. In my mind what was coming to me was four and a half. I didn't understand it at the time. It was exactly four and a half years later I discovered what was done to Joseph.

I thought the world of the hospital, even though Joseph didn't make it through surgery. I always believed that they did their best for him. I couldn't praise them enough. I did a lot of fundraising for the hospital. I organised a charity walk. After me praising the hospital so much I convinced my colleagues at work to donate a pound of their wages every week. In all, I raised over £13,000 for the hospital.

That September we went up to Dublin for his post-mortem reading. I again asked if any of his organs might have been available for donation. Again I was told, 'Nothing only his eyes.' I had two children after that.

On 8 December 1999 my husband and I were watching the News at 6 p.m. I saw Fionnuala O'Reilly on the News and heard her claim that her child's organs had been harvested at a Dublin hospital. I said it couldn't be true but I rang the hospital and asked for an appointment. On 10 December I met with a senior staff member in that hospital. I bluntly asked if Joseph's organs had been retained. The answer I got was, 'His heart was retained.'

I responded, 'Where is it?'

'It was incinerated six months after his death.'

I met up with Fionnuala O'Reilly on 16 December and we had a meeting with the then Minister for Health, Brian Cowen, and medical staff in the department. The meeting lasted two and a half hours. My impression was that the minister was totally shocked. He told us that we would get all the information we needed.

I asked for Joseph's medical files in December and I got them on 7 January 2000. As we went through them we discovered that there were some other children's names, Christian and surnames, in his medical files. One child was a patient at the same time as Joseph but had a different surname and came from a very different part of the country and had a completely different diagnosis. The other child was only in hospital for a day but had the same surname, though a different Christian name.

On 13 January I asked to see Joseph's original files. The same names were there as well. As I was going through his files a doctor said to me, 'Are you looking for his ICU charts?' Of course I said I was. It was through them that I discovered that Joseph had died in intensive care and not in theatre as I had been led to believe all those years. Then I was told that he had haemorrhaged.

That same day I also discovered that Joseph's lungs had been taken. On 10 December I had been assured that only his heart had been taken.

My husband and I met with senior staff and the main surgeon in the hospital on 4 February to explain to us the whole procedure about Joseph and why his organs were retained. We asked the surgeon if at the time he was speaking to us the day after Joseph's death he knew that Joseph's organs would be retained. He tried every way he could not to answer the question. I kept repeating the question but each time he tried to change the subject. He finally answered after approximately ten to fifteen minutes, 'Yes, I did know.' Those were the words from the man's mouth.

We asked him if he was certain that Joseph's heart had been incinerated six months after his death. He told us that it might have been transported to Holland. They can't prove what organs went out.

They also told us that it takes between three to four weeks to finalise the results of the post-mortem and to establish the cause of death. My husband asked if it took three to four weeks to finalise a post-mortem report, how come his death was registered three days after his death, with the cause of death on his death certificate. At that stage we showed them Joseph's death certificate, which was registered three days after his death by a senior staff member in the hospital. They nearly dropped when they saw the document. They could not answer any question after that.

We actually got two different death certificates for Joseph. The first is made out for Joseph James Butler. The second is made out for James Joseph Butler.

The hospitals have been telling families they could not tell parents because of the grief and upset they were going through at the time their child died, but I gave them the golden opportunity of telling me that they did retain organs belonging to Joseph. In fact, I gave them the opportunity to tell me on two occasions. They had no excuse not to tell me.

Since then we've had a constant battle to get the facts out of the hospital. On 28 August 2000 I received a letter from the hospital, which included the following admission:

> During your recent telephone conversation you queried whether Joseph's kidneys were removed during the post-mortem. I'm advised that the post-mortem report indicates that Joseph's kidneys were examined. To the best of my knowledge, information and belief we have no written record of where the kidneys were retained. However, it has been confirmed to me that a sample of tissue or biopsy was retained from Joseph's kidney and this was preserved in a wax block from which a microscopic slide was prepared. This is one of twelve wax blocks and related slides in relation to Joseph's post-mortem. They are held as a part of the hospital's records in relation to Joseph.

I only got this information by wearing them down for eight months. The attitude of the hospital staff to me has been very cold.

I hope for the future that no parent will ever go through what we have been through with the hospital and we hope that all the doctors in the state and in the world will understand parents. These parents have the right to speak on behalf of their own children.

I just hope that nobody has made a profit out of my son's organs.

Patrick

In 1985 Josephine and Pat Cleere's first child, Patrick, was born at 11.30 p.m. on 1 May. He had anacephelia and was born with virtually no skull. He survived three hours. A vast number of Patrick's organs were retained without his parents' consent. Although time is supposed to heal all wounds, the Cleeres are still incredulous about the way they and their first child were treated by the medical profession.

> When we found out fifteen years after our son's death that Patrick's organs had been retained, it was just adding insult to injury because of the way we had been treated at the time of his birth and death. Josephine had several scans during her pregnancy. Although there was never mention of anything wrong, yet we are certain they knew. When Josephine went into labour she was told bluntly that 'your child is deformed and won't live'. We told them that we wanted to see our child regardless of what his deformities were or whether he was dead or not. We were very, very clear that we wanted to see our child. We were instructed to tell relatives phoning during labour that the child was already dead.

Josephine takes up the story.

> At birth the staff who delivered him whipped him out of the room the instant that he was born and only returned him to us after strong protest, saying he was dead and, 'You don't want to see him.' After much insisting by us, they announced they had found a heartbeat. They told us that they wanted to christen him and asked us if we had a name for him. We said: 'Patrick'. They brought him to us. He seemed quite conscious although it was certain that death was only minutes or hours away at best. They let us hold him for a few minutes, approximately five, then took him away from us. Those few minutes have had to do us forever.

Pat recalls the next sequence of events clearly.

> They said they'd take him 'somewhere he'd be more
> comfortable'. When we asked where that was they basically
> wouldn't answer the question. I asked if I could stay with the
> baby but I was told that I could not. When I asked again I was
> told that I could not and would not be accommodated in the
> hospital. I was in so much shock that I did as I was told and
> went home. Josephine was brought to a room and sedated
> despite our protests that we wanted to be with him.

Did you wish to be sedated, Josephine?

> No. I did not.

To add insult to injury, there was another source of annoyance for Pat.

> Josephine was given a Polaroid photo of the baby which was not
> very clear since she could not see the baby's face. She requested
> another, to be told, 'We only give one.'

There was another episode that caused serious disquiet to Josephine.

> Before going to sleep I asked to be woken after a short sleep to
> be with Patrick. This did not happen. I asked if Patrick would
> have a post-mortem. They said yes, and I requested that no
> post-mortem take place before I had a chance to be with the
> child. When I awoke at 6 a.m. approximately, I asked to see
> Patrick, to be told he had died around 2.30 and was now having
> a post-mortem. It is important to note that neither of us recall
> being asked for permission for the post-mortem.
>
> To this day neither of us knows where Patrick was kept in the
> hospital or if he died alone.
>
> We subsequently received two other photos of Patrick after
> the post-mortem had been carried out. Because of this, we asked
> my mother to take some photographs for us in the hospital the
> next day.

Pat's concerns that his child may have been denied dignity in life were exacerbated by his belief that his son was denied dignity in death.

> His coffin was carried out in a holdall bag when it was time to take his remains out of the hospital.
>
> Patrick was laid out in a cardboard box. We have a photo to prove the same. We had no opportunity to hold Patrick or dress him for burial, in fact, a nun in the hospital insisted that a vest was adequate for Patrick for burial and we argued for the clothing we wished to be placed on him. We eventually won this 'concession'.
>
> On removal of the remains we were refused entry to the car park, being told, 'for staff only'. We had to park on a yellow line across from the main entrance.
>
> The coffin was removed from the hospital in a holdall bag which was brought to us by a hospital porter (door man) who accompanied us to the car via the lift and out the front door. He waited while the coffin was placed in the car and retrieved the hospital holdall bag. This (removal by holdall bag) has been denied by the hospital at a recent public meeting with the minister but we have a photo to prove it took place.
>
> All empathy was with mothers yet to deliver and anything we succeeded in gaining from the hospital was through insistence and argument.
>
> I have carried the guilt of deserting my son all these years.

Fifteen years later Josephine would have to relive these painful memories again.

> In January 2000, following reports in the media, Pat investigated if Patrick's organs had been retained. It was confirmed that yes they had.
>
> The hospital retained most of Patrick's organs without our knowledge or consent for fifteen years. This added to our feelings that we had somehow failed to protect our child. We retrieved Patrick's organs on 7 April this year and interred them with him.

We refused the hospital offers of funeral arrangements, a prayer service and a casket. We paid for the casket ourselves, brought it home ourselves and performed our own ceremony. We believe the offer of the hospital to be hypocritical in the extreme, since his organs were preserved on a shelf for fifteen years and meant nothing to them for that length of time and now they wanted us to have a ceremony when it suited them. We also carried our child's remains out the front door in full view of everybody because we refused to hide the issue away for the hospital's sake. We do not wish to upset others but it helped us to restore our child's dignity a certain amount.

We believe the hospital's wishes were paramount in this entire situation and all attempts were made to make our wishes subordinate to those of the medical staff.

Patrick's brain tissue was not returned to us, even though we know it has been examined.

The ironic thing is that the Cleeres would have been willing to donate Patrick's organs if they had been asked.

In spite of the way we were treated we would have been very willing to donate his organs.

Did the question ever arise?

Absolutely not.

While Irish public opinion was profoundly shocked by the organ harvesting scandal, more was to follow.

Children at Risk

On 6 April 2000 the *Irish Times* reported that testing of vaccines on residents of children's homes in the 1960s and 1970s may have been done without the consent of parents or guardians and may have left some children susceptible to serious illness. The *Irish Times* detailed how a home in Bessboro, County Cork, an area now covered by the Southern Health Board, was one of the venues where the effectiveness of a polio vaccine when added to the traditional three-in-one vaccine was tested. In all, seventy-eight children at the home aged less than one year were reported to have been vaccinated there and they appear to have been part of the trial. Of the children vaccinated, twenty-three started and twenty completed treatment with the quadruple vaccine. Vaccine trials also took place in children's homes run by religious orders in the then Dublin Health Authority area. Under legislation introduced in 1987, such trials could not proceed without the consent of parents or guardians. These studies were in line with the ethical guidelines of the Irish Medical Council.

On 9 November 2000 a Government report on three trials of vaccines on close to 200 children – 118 of them in children's homes – revealed that Irish orphans in children's homes were used in commercial trials by drug companies to test new vaccines. The report stated that the tests on the vaccines may have left some of the children susceptible to serious illness. In particular, they contend that some children used in one trial may have been more susceptible to polio infection as a result of being given the trial vaccine. The report was critical of the absence of documentation in the trials.

Speaking in the Dáil, the Minister for Health, Mr Micheál Martin, stated that the report left a number of unanswered questions, including:

> What rationale led to the decision that children not in the State's care got the regular vaccine and children in the State's care got the variant? Was the end result from each trial for the public good or for the commercial advantage of a manufacturer? Why were some medications given to children who were outside the age group at which these medications were known to be effective? Above all, we must ask why the records of some of the trials are so woefully inadequate at almost every point?

There are special problems with experiments that are performed upon children in orphanages, reformatories, or homes for the severely intellectually challenged because they are a captive population. In 1958 and 1959, for example, the *New England Journal of Medicine* reported on a number of experiments performed upon patients and new admittees to the Willowbrook State School, a home for intellectually challenged children in Staten Island, New York. These experiments were described as 'an attempt to control the high prevalence of infectous hepatitis in an institution for mentally defective patients'. The official justification for the experiments was that under conditions of an existing controlled outbreak of hepatitis in the institution, 'knowledge obtained from a series of suitable studies could well lead to its control'. In practice, the experiments were intended to duplicate and confirm the efficacy of gamma globulin in immunisation against hepatitis, to develop and improve upon that inoculum, and to learn more about infectious hepatitis in general.

Clearly, parental responsibility is weakened when children are institutionalised, when their offspring are no longer directly and continously under their care. One of the major ethical concerns about this study was that, while there were 4478 children at Willowbrook, there was no apparent effort to recruit any of the 1000 adult staff who could easily have given a valid consent to it. There is nothing that obliges a major research into the natural history of hepatitis be first undertaken in children.

Pharmaceutical firms are closely involved in the sponsorship of clinical research. This is inevitable in the light of the costs of such research and the limited scope for public funding of academic research. Governments actively encourage the close partnership of universities and commercial organisations. It is expected that society as a whole stands to benefit in consequence. However, there are dangers in relying on commercial involvement in the development of medical research and technology. An obvious danger is that through such involvements, researchers will face a conflict of interest.

Conflicts of interest occur in circumstances where a person's private interest conflicts actually or potentially with a fiduciary duty connected with the person's occupational or professional role. The private interests need not be mercenary and need not be personal – one might have a private interest in helping a friend or in harming an enemy. Such conflicts are commonplace in both commercial and non-commercial settings. Conflicts of interest occur not just where a person deviates from duty on account of the private interest. Even if a person is unaffected, undiverted, by the private interest, there is harm in allowing the conflict to continue. Trust will inevitably be undermined wherever there is potential for conflict of interest.

Trust in the medical profession has been undermined by the recent scandals. If 1700 children in the Dublin area alone have had their organs harvested without their parents' consent, there are serious questions that must be confronted. Before attempting to address the issues raised by the Irish experience, perhaps we could benefit from a study of the experience in other countries.

Across the Nations
Under the Danish legislation on transplantation, for example, the next-of-kin have decisive influence over whether a possible donor is in fact used as a donor. If the relatives say no, organ donation cannot take place, even if the deceased agreed to donate while alive. Other countries have legislation that is based on 'presumed consent', i.e., it is presumed that a deceased person would have given consent for organ donation if the deceased had not actively declined to do so while alive. In some of the countries it is not necessary to ask the relatives for permission to perform the transplant. In countries where variations on the 'presumed consent' approach were tried, organ donation rates did not improve significantly. An acute shortage of kidney donations has led to calls for a change in the rules of consent in Britain. Against this backdrop the British Medical Association has advocated an opt-out rule to replace the current system, facilitating easier donation.

Hungary accepts presumed consent in regard to organ transplantation: the organs of dead people can be harvested unless they have explicitly prohibited this during their lifetime. If they have not done so, their surviving relatives cannot prohibit it. Accordingly, if a physician does not find such a prohibition in the patient's record, they can remove any organ of the corpse without being obliged even to ask a relative. Critics query whether presumed consent can be accepted as real consent or whether it is a subtle form of coercing people into becoming organ donors after their death.

They also contend that people in Hungary know very little about the current law and about the possibility of being a potential organ donor after their death. They are unaware that they have to prohibit the removal of their organs after their death in order not to become organ donors. In this perspective, presumed consent could only be ethical if there were extensive media coverage of organ transplantation in general, so that people would become aware of their options under the current law.

Hungarian transplantation surgeons in the main resolutely oppose any media coverage of these issues. They contend that the result of any such information campaign could only be that more people will explicitly prohibit removal of their organs after death. They also argue that even under the system of presumed consent the number of kidney transplantations is very small due to a shortage of transplantable organs, and any constrictions of the transplantation law would precipitate a further drop of transplantable organs, which would be calamitous.

These physicians maintain that their ultimate responsibility is towards living patients who desperately require a transplantable organ, and not towards corpses. According to this critique, to remove an organ from a corpse is very similar to autopsy. In Hungary autopsies are obligatory in some cases; and as nobody protests against this practice, it is illogical to protest against presumed consent for organ donation. They contend that the removal of transplantable organs from corpses must be considered as a form of autopsy in the public's interest. Relatively few Hungarians seek explicit consent. Opponents of presumed consent only want to improve it by making much more information available for the public about the practice of harvesting organs.

Informed consent does not feature in Hungarian medical practice. Up to 1990 their law requested doctors to inform patients about their diagnosis and prognosis honestly, but tactfully. This law, however, permitted an exception. It allowed doctors not to disclose information, if such information would be detrimental to the patient. This exception was so routinely abused by the medical profession, that it was abolished from the new law in 1990. According to the new law, doctors have no legal possibility whatsover to fail to divulge any information to the patient. However, the new law made no real impact on medical practice. Hungarian doctors seldom inform terminally ill patients, for example, of the true state of their health.

Organ transplantations from brain-dead patients are now commonplace in many developed countries, but they still remain a taboo in Japan because of the lack of a national consensus. This is despite the report of a governmental commission in January 1992 on the issue of brain death and organ transplantation, which allowed organ transplantations from brain-dead patients. However, no transplantations had been done up to a study in September 1993, and the police authorities are still adopting the cardio-pulmonary criteria of death in coroner's inquests. Although more than half of respondents to public opinion polls approved organ transplantation from brain-dead patients, many ardent opponents remain. The reluctance of Japanese people to accepting brain death as the death of a person can be attributed to the following:

1. A distrust of practitioners. The first heart transplantation in Japan was performed in 1968 by a Professor Wada. However, strong doubts emerged regarding the diagnosis of brain death of the donor and the surgical indication for the operation of the recipient. Consequently Professor Wada was accused of murder. Since that incident, popular mistrust in the physicians who intend to do organ transplantations has grown, and surgeons have kept away from doing transplantations from brain-dead patients because of the fear of being sued.
2. Distinctions between relatives and strangers. Many parents have donated a kidney or parts of the liver to their children. However, few people have registered in the donor-card system, which is intended for organ transplantations to anonymous non-relatives.
3. Priority of families to individuals. Under the principle of informed consent the decision of the individual has priority over all other agents. The situation in Japan is that individuals are subject to the decision of their families, even when they have decided to donate their organs.
4. Attachment to the remains. For example, when relatives are lost in airplane accidents, Japanese people are known to go to great lengths to retrieve even a tiny part of the remains. Their belief is that the soul resides in every part of the remains, so that the

removal of organs prior to funeral is repugnant to the traditional sensitivities of the Japanese people.

5. Feeling of reluctance based on the common sense. They see a brain-dead person and find it difficult to believe that this warm, pulsating body is really dead. It goes against their ordinary idea of death.

6. A gradual acceptance of the death on the part of relatives. The diagnosis of death does not necessarily mean that the death is accepted by relatives. When death is diagnosed by the doctor, there begins a long series of rituals that help people to realise gradually that the deceased is gone forever. Accordingly, it goes against their culture to identify the diagnosis of brain death with the death of the person.

One argument that is sometimes advocated in public discourse on organ transplants is that there is a shortage of organs for transplanting and this deficiency might be circumvented with laxer rules of consent. Lax consent laws, however, will not meet the demand for organs, nor will they solve the problem of waiting lists. Firstly, it appears that the more organs we procure, the greater will be the demand for organ donation. This is because the indications for organ transplantation as a method of treatment will change, as medical practitioners will perceive transplantation as a solution to more health problems. In that sense the demand for organs will invariably be one step ahead of the supply of organs for transplants.

Secondly, the rules of consent, regardless of their nature, are not the defining issue in the number of organs offered for donation. There is international data to indicate that explicit consent systems decrease availability of organs. However, the international experience is that various types of organisational initiatives have a greater bearing on the number of organs procured. Some of these initiatives raise ethical questions. There is anecdotal evidence that in Spain, for example, staff are paid in relation to the number of organs they obtain. If financial inducements are offered for medical staff to obtain organs, that would greatly call into question whether the next-of-kin even have the possibility of providing non-directed, informed consent for organ donation.

The Report of the Conference of European Health Ministers of November 1987 stated:

> The sale of human organs is no longer a myth and the wealthiest can buy life at the expense of the most underprivileged. That is where we have been led by an act of which ethics approves, and we are only at the beginning of venture fraught with dangers. Organ donation is undoubtedly a profoundly humane gesture, but its legislation and use without major restrictions involve one of the greatest risks man has ever run, that of giving a value to his body, a price to his life.

As if to prove their point, in 1990 the British Medical Council banned Raymond Crockett from practising after he arranged for kidneys to be removed from four people in Turkey who received between £2,500 and £3,500 for the organs. He transplanted the kidneys into private patients who had been turned down for transplants by the NHS. They paid £66,000 for the operations at the Wellington Humana Hospital in St John's Wood, North London.

The Restriction of Risk and the Risk of Restriction

Since the Nuremberg Trials, the code of ethics for medical research is firmly anchored on the concept of informed consent. The Helsinki Accords underscore the importance of individual rights as a check on the power of modern medicine, as well as the creation of a partnership between doctors and patients in advancing medical knowledge.

Problems constantly arise with the concept of informed consent, particularly in relation to what counts as sufficient information and what counts as true consent without some form of coercion. In the 1990s some exceptions to informed consent were approved in the United States. These exceptions relate to potentially beneficial research on currently incompetent patients, e.g. due to trauma head injury. In order to proceed, this research must be widely publicised in the community from which patients are drawn.

Pascal once wrote of 'the Right Use of Sickness'. Historically, experimental medicine has been something of a minefield. In the

Western world the Hippocratic tradition has always emphasised the principle *primum non nocere* (first do no harm). In other words, the interests of the patient must always prevail over the interests of society. The World Medical Association's 1975 declaration on the subject reiterated that sentiment. However, in practice ethical decisions in medicine are much hazier; the good of the patient is not an end in itself. There could not have been the advances in such areas as chemotherapy and kidney transplants if health-care professionals had not taken account of possible benefits to future patients. How, though, are doctors to strike the correct balance between the interests of the individual patient and the good of society? What constraints should there be on doctors working in this area? How much risk should a patient be reasonably expected to face? Should experimental techniques be turned to only as a last resort, or much earlier if they offer a reasonable chance of life to the patient?

The *Helsinki II Declaration* on biomedical research on human subjects tilts the balance firmly in favour of the individual:

> Every precaution must be taken to minimise the effect of the research project on the testee's physical and mental integrity and personality. . . . Regard for the interest of the researchee must always be put before the interests of research or society. . . . In research on humans, research and the interests of society should never take precedence over consideration for the well-being of the testee. . . . The right of the testee to protect his/her integrity must at all times be respected.

In this context it is worth noting that in 1982 Pope John Paul II gave an address to biological researchers. He claimed that the whole human person, spirit and body, is the ultimate goal of scientific research, even if the immediate object of the sciences is the body, with all its organs and tissues. He went on to argue that the human body is not independent of the spirit, in the same way the spirit is not independent of the body, in the light of the deep unity and mutual connection that exist between one and the other. He stressed the importance of scientific and medical research that promotes knowledge of the corporeal reality and activity for the life of the spirit.

Other Christian Churches too have spoke out in this area. In 1984 the Lutheran Church in America passed a resolution stating that organ donation contributes to the well-being of humanity and can be 'an expression of sacrificial love for a neighbour in need'. They call on 'members to consider donating organs and to make any necessary family and legal arrangements, including the use of a signed donor card'. The United Methodist Church also issued a policy statement on this matter: 'The United Methodist Church recognizes the life-giving benefits of organ and tissue donation, and thereby encourages all Christians to become organ and tissue donors by signing and carrying cards or driver's licenses, attesting to their commitment of such organs upon their death, to those in need, as a part of their ministry to others in the name of Christ, who gave His life that we might have life in its fullness'.

As in the case of all professional activity, regulation is necessary. In establishing those controls, it is necessary to weigh fully the possible resultant losses. While the restriction of risk ought to be a priority in research, there is also a risk of restriction, i.e. there are dangers of not doing research. Doctors do their best to save children at risk of dying using drugs and treatments that were devloped following postmortems on those who had gone to their eternal reward before. Without the knowledge that is carefully collated from these procedures, attempts to discover new and better treatments will be jeopardised. Many of the children whose organs were harvested in Irish hospitals died because of illnesses that still require further investigative studies for causes and potential treatments. In those circumstances many parents would be willing to donate some of their children's tissue to prevent further babies dying in the future.

Autopsies serve diagnostic, teaching and research functions. Postmortems can chart not only the cause of death but also the response of disease to treatment, and for families may also highlight co-existing conditions, such as inheritable problems, whose early detection may be beneficial to other family members. Data gained from post-mortem examinations can benefit society in a number of ways – for assessing and enhancing the quality of medical care; for research into the character, causes and prevention of disease; for the ongoing development of doctors present and future; and for public health planning by furnishing exact mortality and morbidity statistics.

One of the difficulties of the discussion is that the advantages to the person and the advantages to the community are not always the same. The obvious question that arises is: what risks are justifiable for the sake of possibly great gains? Accordingly, some researchers have challenged the so-called golden rule of medical ethics: 'First do no harm'. Instead they argue for an adaption of the phrase on the lines of: 'Be willing to do some harm that greater good may come'. However, despite the apparent attractiveness of this approach, particularly in terms of keeping costs to a minimum, it effectively allows people to be treated as means to an end.

Because science is incomplete and reason is imperfect, both are open to abuse. However, it is not research but the misapplication of research that crosses the ethical red light. It is not knowledge but ignorance that guarantees the continuation of human misery. The ethical questions become political questions. Who shall control the products of this research? For what purpose shall they be employed? Having earlier protested about the dangers of Louis Pasteur's research, the citizens of France, by public subscriptions in gratitude for his contribution to the good of humankind, erected the Pasteur Institute. So moved was Pasteur at the ceremony of dedication that he asked his son to read his remarks. The address concluded as follows:

> Two opposing laws seem now to be in contest. The one, a law of blood and death, ever imagining new means of destruction, forces nations always to be ready for battle. The other, a law of peace, work and health, ever evolving means of delivering man from the scourges which beset him. The one seeks violent conquests, the other the relief of humanity. The one places a single life above all victories, the other sacrifices hundreds of thousands of lives to the ambition of a single individual. The law of which we are the instruments strives even in the midst of carnage to cure the wounds due to the law of war. Treatment by our antiseptic methods may save the lives of thousands of soldiers. Which of these two laws will ultimately prevail, God

alone knows. But this we may assert: that French science will have tried, by obeying the law of Humanity, to extend the frontiers of life.

Light out of darkness

Controversy erupted in October 1994 when the authorities at a leading Catholic school in England, Ampleforth College, pulled out of the Government's measles immunisation programme because parts of the vaccine came from an aborted foetus. A number of parents considered the death of the foetus to be ethically significant in terms of their decision to vaccinate their children. They assumed that by agreeing to the vaccination they were accomplices to abortion by association.

The British Chief Medical Officer explained that:

> Most vaccines were not grown on any human material but in cell culture whose cells are called MRCR. This cell line was developed from a small number of cells taken from a single foetus in 1966 and the cells have grown and replicated since then and been used widely for growing viruses. The termination of pregnancy was carried out on medical grounds in a National Health Service hospital and no further foetal material has been involved since 1966. The attenuated viruses that are grown in these MRCR cells are subsequently highly purified and so the vaccine does not contain any foetal tissue.

The Royal College of Nursing instructed Catholic nurses to carry out the measles vaccination, claiming that any nurse who refused to do so would be guilty of professional negligence. A statement for the Joint Bioethics Committee of the Roman Catholic Bishops of England, Wales, Scotland and Ireland said that consenting to vaccination did not condone abortion or encourage further abortions, and claimed: 'The substantial benefits of this vaccine, for which there is no substitute available, may be accepted'. This thoughtful and nuanced approach is an excellent example of the kind of ethical discourse that takes account of the particular and elucidates without recourse to cheap slogans. Hopefully it could herald in a new style of ethical reasoning in this thorny area.

As to the wider issue of the use of aborted foetal tissue in medicines, a number of points need to be made. This issue did not fall from the heavens in 1994. In 1954 John Enders and Thomas Weller were presented with the Nobel Prize for successfully culturing the poliomyelitis virus in cells grown from human foetal tissue. Their work in this field in 1928, which led to the development of the polio vaccine, was the first breakthrough in research using human foetal tissue. Subsequently, human foetal tissue has been used to increase medical knowledge and to treat a variety of medical conditions. Foetal cells have certain properties that make them more effective than adult equivalents. Foetal cells are easily cultured, reproduce rapidly and can be less antigenic than adult tissue, making immunological rejection by a recipient less probable. Moreover, foetal tissue is in greater supply than any other human tissue due to the availability of elective abortion in many countries.

In assessing the ethical significance of foetal tissue in health care we must first distinguish between committing moral evil solely for the purpose of obtaining a favourable outcome, and salvaging good from tragic or ethically questionable circumstances. The development of the rubella vaccine falls into the latter category. The scientists who made use of the vaccine were not ethically responsible for the abortion; they deployed otherwise incinerated tissue for the benefit of humankind.

In some cases good can come from evil. Our knowledge of radiation sickness and its treatment has been gained, to a significant degree, from the effects of the Hiroshima and Nagasaki nuclear bombings in 1945. This knowledge was not expected and was not a factor in the decision to drop the bombs. It cannot be assumed that those who have been treated for radiation sickness approve of the decision to drop the bomb. Likewise, the medical treatment of hypothermia in use today was based on knowledge gained by cruel Nazi experiments on non-consenting human subjects. Despite the barbarism of the Nazis, people should not refuse treatment for hypothermia, since ethical disapproval of circumstances that give rise to benefit need not preclude the possibility of utilising those benefits for the good of humankind. No refusal to accept treatment for hypothermia can ever undo the cruelty of the Nazis. What is ethically reprehensible is the belief that the evil committed was a price worth paying. Our chief ethical task is to try to ensure that this type of abuse never happens again. Sadly, the reports from Amnesty International suggest that such abuses are still a fact of life in some parts of the world.

Medical research is a noble ideal. The problem, though, in the cases we have examined is that the means used in its name compromised these lofty ideals.

There is public goodwill towards organ donation. In February 2000 when an RTÉ drama series, *Relative Strangers,* portrayed the fictional death of a child when a compatible donor could not be found to give him a life-saving bone-marrow transplant, it led to over a hundred calls to the Blood Transfusion Service Board from members of the public interested in becoming bone-marrow donors, more than the total received during the whole of the previous year. However, goodwill can evaporate very quickly and the medical profession needs to do its utmost to nurture this goodwill. The public must recognise that research is necessary and desirable once there are appropriate safeguards.

New Guidelines

In February 2000 the Faculty of Pathology of the Royal College of Physicians of Ireland issued revised guidelines on post-mortem practices in the aftermath of the public disquiet about the harvesting of children's organs. With commendable honesty they acknowledge in the introduction: 'Current practice in autopsy pathology was developed many years ago at a time when medical practice was paternalistic and when the principles of informed consent were less developed'.

These guidelines offer many invaluable practical signposts in this area. The section on consent includes the following:

> Pathologists have a duty of education to medical, nursing and paramedical staff about the purpose and nature of autopsy practice to facilitate informed discussion with relatives at the

time of death. . . . Consent for use of tissue for teaching and/or research should be specifically sought. . . . Consultant pathology staff should be available for either direct or indirect discussion with relatives if further clarification about any post-mortem issues is required. As not all relatives will wish to discuss this difficult and sensitive area, information may be given in a staggered or step-wise fashion, for example, by asking 'do you wish to have any more information about the post-mortem examination?'

There are also helpful sections on: Limited Post-mortems; Coroner's Post-mortems; Retention of Organs and Tissues; Research; Coroner's cases; and Coroner's Autopsy. In the light of the mistakes of the past, the section on Next-of-Kin is particularly interesting:

Permission for a non-coroner's autopsy examination must be sought from the next-of-kin. The medical staff seeking consent should satisfy themselves that no closer relatives (who may therefore have a superior right over the disposition of the body) exist. Similarly, they should be satisfied that the patient has not made a living will specifically precluding a post-mortem.

Mindful of recent history, the section on the Ultimate Disposition of Retained Organs has a noteworthy line: 'The ultimate disposition of organs retained at post-mortem should reflect, where possible, the wishes of the individual family'.

The guidelines also explored the discussions on the many complexities and sensitivities in this area in Britain, spearheaded by the Royal College of Pathologists. The four key emphases are:

1. Obtaining a truly informed consent to perform an autopsy. In particular, it has been stated that it is no longer acceptable to say that certain details were not given to relatives of the deceased in order to avoid causing them further distress.
2. Indicating that the permission sought is to make an examination to find the cause of death, the nature and extent of disease and the effects of therapy.

3. Obtaining further permission if tissue or organs are to be used for research or teaching.
4. Clearly stating what tissues or organs have been retained and defining how they will be disposed of.

Never Again

As we have seen, great distress was caused to parents and families as the steady stream of revelations about past events emerged. The practice of harvesting organs without the consent of parents may have been prompted by a good intention, i.e. to save relatives from additional distress. Understandably, from a purely human point of view, doctors are reluctant to ask parents distraught with grief at the loss of a child for permission to carry out a post-mortem examination immediately after the child's death. However, it represents another glaring example of the problem of paternalism, albeit benign, in the medical profession. Even if the intention was honourable, how could the storage and disposal of such organs be handled so insensitively? This problem is accentuated by the fact that many relatives remain distressed by their lack of knowledge of what happened to these organs. The communications failure is compounded by the lack of an adequate system to establish what happened to these organs after examination and how they were disposed of ultimately.

What can be done to ensure that organs are adequately and sensitively managed in the future? Legislation is required as a matter of urgency. A carefully defined Human Tissues Act must clearly detail how organs should be handled when they are retained at post-mortem. In the circumstances, those entrusted with drawing up this legislation should consider the insights of Parents for Justice.

It is neither my task nor my wish to adjudicate on the professionals involved in this controversy. I am very mindful of the Latin maxim *actus non facit reus, nisi sit mens rea.* Roughly translated, this means 'the act does not make the person guilty without the presence of a guilty mind'. However, the controversy highlights glaring inadequacies in the profession's regard for patient's autonomy.

Autonomy is always a matter of degree. It is seldom fully present or absent in the decisions and actions of peoples and groups. The harrowing experiences of many people in this area requires that there be clear and unambiguous legislation with regard to the consent requirements in Irish law. There ought to be respect for both the deceased and the next-of-kin's wishes in relation to organ donation, and these considerations must be reasonably balanced in any legislation. We must avoid a situation in future that entails confrontations between relatives and medical staff, which will be ethically acceptable to no one. However, we also require a new culture in the medical profession that sees patient autonomy elevated to a more central role in medical practice. It is my task in the following chapter to consider this issue more fully.

2

DOCTOR KNOWS BEST?

There is a story told about St Francis of Assisi that illustrates the problem of blind obedience. One day two young men came to Francis, saying that they wanted to join his friars. Francis looked at them and said, 'Before accepting you, I would like you to do something for me.' As he said this, he stooped down, picked up two cabbage plants and handed one to each of the two men. Pointing to a small patch of newly dug soil, he asked them to plant the cabbages. They were about to do this, when Francis added, 'there is just one more thing. I want you to plant them upside down, with the leaves buried and the roots in the air.' Immediately one of the men picked up a trowel and did what Francis directed. The other politely pointed out that if the cabbages were planted like that they would never grow. This prospective monk was asked to return home while the first man was enthusiastically welcomed into the brotherhood. In the past, patients have given virtual blind obedience to doctors.

Clinicians have status, knowledge and experience in their specialist area and, accordingly, may seem formidable to the patient. In contrast, the patient is vulnerable and, relatively speaking, ignorant. Of course this is not unique to the doctor-patient relationship. In most professional-client relationships there is a similar imbalance of power. How do doctors themselves feel that this power should be exercised? Leonard Condren is a GP in Ballyfermot and is former Medical Editor of *Forum*. He feels the medical profession's reputation has been damaged by the organ-harvesting scandal.

> I think the profession has come out of it badly and I think our colleagues in pathology have let the profession down rather badly. When the story first emerged a senior person in pathology should have seen the potential for the controversy to

develop a momentum that would take it into a whole load of areas that it didn't need to go to at all. I think the practice of organ retention can be defended and all the work they do after post-mortems can be justified. I don't think the failure in the 'scandal' was one of practice but a failure of communication, where people should have come out quickly and said what was happening and why it was happening.

In fact, what happened was they retreated into the bunker and waited for all the noise to pass over and then re-emerged again as if nothing had happened, but their failure to talk and explain the situation has done a great disservice to the public. This story has taken legs and run in five or six directions all at once and the ripples in the pond have not been what the profession wanted. If the story had been handled differently there could have been a positive outcome.

I don't think it surprising that the pathologists have dealt with the situation the way they did. They actually don't interface much with their colleagues at all, let alone interface with the public. They're not in the business much of communication. They are thought of by their colleagues as the brightest members of their profession. To become a pathologist is very difficult, with very hard exams to pass, and it's generally the people with the highest points who become pathologists. They are sort of sidelined in labs, or post-mortem rooms, looking down microscopes or doing electron micrographs and that kind of thing. It is quite conceivable for a pathologist to practise in Dublin without ever meeting a patient. I think perhaps because of the nature of the job they do and the rather rarefied milieu they operate in it's not surprising that they didn't see the potential for this because they are not interacting with the public.

One other difficulty in relation to organ retention is that very often the wrong people are actually talking to relatives at what is a very sensitive time for people. Take for example a fatal road accident if a doctor needs to talk to relatives where there is an issue of organ donation, let alone organ retention for post-mortem purposes, it requires a very skilled person in terms of empathising with people in their predicament. It's of enormous benefit to people that organs are harvested, but that is not explained to the public. It's such a difficult area that it should be the most senior person that has that task, not the most junior person in the hierarchy.

What I'm afraid of is that we're going to be in a worse situation in the future, because what I believe will happen is when people are most traumatised they will be handed a form without a process of discussion that must accompany it. Handing people a piece of paper for them to sign falls far short of what I consider to be informed consent.

If it's not too inappropriate I would like to contrast it with the process I would go through in sterilisation counselling. For example, in vasectomy counselling, before you get into signing the consent form there is a preamble and there are a series of areas you go through. The signing of the consent form is not the start but the culmination of a long process. I think this is one area of medical practice where informed consent works very well. The reason it is necessary is that in the early stages of tubal ligation or vasectomy the procedure wasn't properly discussed. People had understandings about the procedure that didn't conform with the facts.

In general practice a lot of the time the consent is assumed. In most situations for me, the context in which it is happening is that I know the patient for years and what happens is more a matter of negotiation and discussion than the traditional model where the patient presents themselves to the doctor, tells their story and the doctor makes a diagnosis and prescribes medicine. A general practice model is a more fluid and dynamic process than that.

I can give one example of a lady who presented herself to me with symptoms in her chest. She described that she had a cough and slight shortness of breath. This woman had an absolute terror of hospitals. I couldn't find anything seriously wrong with her so we had to negotiate that it would be useful for her to get a chest X-ray, but when she went and had the X-ray the result was that there was a sinister lesion above the heart but it wasn't clear what that was. I discussed it with her but her view was that no, she didn't want to go to hospital and would sooner not know what it was and that she'd rather leave it like that. Years later she is still attending me and she's well, but I'm not sure what's going to happen to her – whether she'll blow a blood vessel or something like that, but there was a permission-consent thing going on there between the various consultations. That would be very different with somebody else coming in with a lesion on their lung – so very often it's a process of negotiation. I believe that every so often it's better to be frank with people but in a sensitive way. Very often doctors can be frank with people but in a brutal way when they just tell them the cold hard facts, in a way that is totally lacking in sensitivity.

Consent should be a matter of negotiation. Sometimes you'd be recommending a particular tablet to people and the patient would be saying: 'I don't like that tablet and anyway I don't much like tablets and could I go to a physiotherapist instead?' Sometimes you'd be saying to people: 'I really do think this would be a better option, but if that's what you want to do, that's what we'll do, because at the end of the day it's important that you be satisfied with the outcome'. We do that and then we take it from there. It's not as controlled and it's not as rigid as the traditional medical model.

I think that a lot of it has to do with the area in which we have to work. We are out there with the patients and we are their first point of contact in the housing estates or shopping centres. There's no waiting list in general practice. If you want to see your GP you can usually see them the same day, certainly within twenty-four hours. You're in that sort of environment and you've got to be accessible to people. The traditional paternalistic approach to medical practice just won't work in that environment.

GPs recognised thirty years ago that the traditional medical model and the skills that people learn in medical school just weren't appropriate for people out in the community. If it is not too inappropriate an analogy, somebody compared it to the difference between a naturalist working in the wild as opposed to a zoologist dealing with animals in the zoo. I think there's an element of truth in that. That's not to say we are providing better medical practice than specialists because they are operating in a different milieu and the level of service we provide would not be appropriate to them nor a good use of their time. Before a patient comes to a specialist they have already gone through a filter with a number of consultations and much of that information has been distilled. Even though the GP may not have an exact diagnosis given, they may have narrowed it down. They may say it's a cardiovascular problem or a respiratory difficulty so that the patient is channelled in that direction. So each model is appropriate to its own environment.

In a sense, in the hospital hierarchy the consultant is God. That scenario couldn't possibly work in general practice. I think that GPs realised quite some time ago that the proper relationship between themselves and patients is one of two adults talking together – rather than transaction analysis, which is an adult talking to a child, which is the traditional model. I should say that it's also possible for a doctor to have an adult conversation with a child because they can spontaneously tell their own story in their own words and often can be very good historians.

The agenda for a consultation should be defined by a patient. You're there to solve their problem so the agenda of the consultation is defined by the patient and not by the doctor. Ultimately, the whole transaction is about addressing what their concerns are. There are a few basic questions in relation to that: What do you think is wrong? What are you afraid might be wrong? What are you expecting me to do about it? These are very different sorts of questions to the traditional ones, i.e. Have you a pain in your chest? Do you have a headache? I think that more and more the colleagues in other aspects of the profession believe that GPs are the communication experts when it comes to consultations. Communication skills have been part of the vocational training for GPs for over thirty years. I believe that everything in general practice stems from the consultation itself. The consultation is the centre of medical practice and everything that happens flows from that.

One barrier to achieving good consent for patients is lack of time. A reasonable tactic is to say to the patient, 'Well there's a lot more here than one can resolve today, but come back tomorrow.' Part of the time, the issue is remuneration. I think all of us should have smaller patient lists where we can give patients more time, but if you're going to have smaller lists you have to be paid more.

I've got a staff including a full-time practice nurse and the equivalent of two full-time practice secretaries. In effect, I have a small business. I've got to be generating a minimum of £60 an hour to be covering my costs, and that's before I start earning a penny for myself. You could have an idyllic practice where you only saw a dozen patients in the morning and a dozen in the afternoon, but to do that you'd need to take vows of poverty, chastity and obedience!

Some days I come home from surgery practically brain dead. I can remember the outbreak of viral illness at Christmas 1999. One morning my wife and I saw sixty-three patients between 8.30 and 1.00. I couldn't remember half of the people I saw because I was just overwhelmed.

On the other hand I had a consultation once when I had a bit of time to spare. A young woman came in to see me. She had constipation, she had abdominal pain and she was feeling tired. I had known her for twenty years and that consultation went into more detail and I discovered that she was having irritable bowel. Then it emerged that there were difficulties with fertility in her marriage. She had had a child before, but her partner hadn't, so in all probability the problem with fertility was his. After a bit into the discussion I discovered that this woman was depressed. She went away with a prescription for an anti-depressant and a much better handle on her problems. I felt pleased afterwards that it had been a good consultation. She had presented with classical physical symptoms but as a result of a dynamic consultation the discussion broadened out and as a result the diagnosis was very different than either of us thought it was going to be at the outset. If I had been under time pressure I probably would have only got a small bit of the way and maybe the opportunity would have been lost.

Threats to the Doctor-Patient Relationship

The need for ongoing ethical reflection in medicine is accentuated by the emergence of new issues in health care. Doctors assume the responsibility for maintaining a broad concern for the patient as person as part of their professional identity. Without high standards of service to the patient, health care runs the risk of succumbing to self-seeking protectionism. Should health care ever become so preoccupied with commercial advantage that the traditional attention to the patient's interests is relegated, would health care cease to be a profession and become nothing more than a business activity?

The changing context of health care highlights the fact that the ethics of the practice of medicine cannot be a static enterprise, otherwise it will simply provide outdated answers to questions that have moved to the periphery of medical practice. Rather, ethical reflection on medicine must consistently seek new and better answers to old questions and grapple seriously with the emerging questions of health care if it is to do justice to its name.

A recurring problem in the area of health care is the conflict between the principles of benefiting the patient and of simultaneously respecting the patient's autonomy. In some conflicts paternalism may ensue. Paternalism is the principle and practice of parental administration; government as by a parent, the claim or attempt to supply the needs or to regulate the life of an individual or group in the same way as a parent does her or his children. The assumption is that the parent acts in the best interests of the child and that the parent makes the majority or all of the decisions necessary to promote the child's welfare. Similarly in the context of medicine, the doctor is considered benevolent and as providing care for the patient (child) incapable of discerning her or his best interests. The health-care professional is pledged to care for the patient. The doctor-patient relationship is distorted when a patient's wishes are simply ignored or over-ridden. In such circumstances, the patient is categorised as subservient, and is thereby denied independence and status as an equal. In effect, the patient is treated as a child, as someone incapable of discriminating between the potential benefit and the potential harm of a course of treatment. Such a situation is abhorrent in the light of the doctor's self-imposed pledge to serve the patient because the patient is effectively enslaved by the professional's notion of the good. However, is every refusal to accept a patient's wishes an assault on the dignity of that patient?

One approach distinguishes between strong and weak paternalism. Two forms of justification that are frequently cited in support of paternalistic interventions are firstly the patient's incapacities and secondly the potential for harm. Where the first of these conditions is deemed to be essential for justified paternalism, the approach is simply that of 'weak' paternalism. Such an approach allows for intervention only in cases where the patient's wishes are not fully voluntary because of some incapacity. 'Strong' paternalism arises when the probability of harm is used to justify paternalism. Intervention is justified when the patient's evaluation of risks and benefits is considered unreasonable, even though this decision is informed and voluntary. Regardless of the nature of the patient's incapacity, intervention can only be justified when it is essential to prevent harm to the patient whose freedom is impaired. Historically, many medical practices presumed paternalism except where questions were raised. In such circumstances, there is an obligation to devise some guidelines as to the occasions in which paternalism is unacceptable. More fundamentally, there is a prior need to consider the autonomy of the patient.

The Autonomy of the Patient
The term 'autonomy' is a composite one, emanating from the Greek words *autos* (self) and *nomos* (rule, governance or law), and was originally employed to refer to self-rule or self-governance in Greek city-states. During the course of the religious wars in Europe,

autonomy was also a claim to confessional self-determination. Today, personal autonomy, in its broadest sense, refers to self-government, being one's own person, without constraints imposed from without.

Autonomy in the sense of self-government is a basic human right, though not a total or absolute one. Moreover, the issue of autonomy is not quite as clear-cut as might be imagined. Public health offers a community justification for paternalistic measures, which, for example, require motorists to wear seat-belts.

Using a similar rationale, the medical profession does not offend personal autonomy when it pursues a campaign to discourage unhealthy practices, e.g. poor diet. Indeed, it might be suggested that the medical profession could honour its commitment to the patient by pursuing such campaigns more aggressively.

In liberal societies with a strong civil rights culture there is an understandable tendency to attach a very high value to personal autonomy. However, ought there be limits to autonomy or should it be an end in itself? Do we allow it to the extent that we tolerate physician-assisted suicide? What about human cloning?

The medical profession may legitimately query patients' or their families' use of automony. In Washington, DC, in the 1990s the doctors caring for baby Rena, an eighteen-month-old in constant pain with AIDS, hydrocephalus, respiratory distress, heart failure and kidney dysfunction, believed that health-care must not be used to torture the dying and they made plans to go to court. Her foster-parents insisted that all treatment must be continued, because God would definitely work a miracle. In these scenarios doctors do not want to be forced into providing treatment that they consider to be medically or ethically wrong.

In the context of health care, the issues of paternalism and autonomy arise most acutely in the area of informed consent.

Let us examine a case loosely based on a recent incident that illustrates the human situations that arise. Seán Murphy is an Irish rugby international who sustains a serious arm injury. He goes to Dr Nolan for a consultation. Dr Nolan recommends major surgery after presenting an exhaustive analysis of Seán's medical condition. Seán has great difficulty in understanding the technical language the doctor uses and believes that by consenting to an operation he will almost certainly make a full recovery. The operation is not a success. Seán sues his doctor on the grounds that he has been misled. The doctor produces her case notes, which establish that Seán has in fact been given all the information he needs. Seán's lawyers argue that while Seán was given the information it was presented in such a way that he could not have understood it sufficiently to give an informed consent. The judge rules against Seán but suggests that Dr Nolan use more 'patient-friendly' language in the future.

Informed Consent

To speak of informed consent is fraught with pitfalls. Can consent ever be totally informed? One argument suggests that the real question is: when is consent 'reasonably free and informed', i.e. sufficiently voluntary and knowledgeable that a reasonable person would consider it adequate? A further approach suggests that 'educated' rather than 'informed' consent represents a more fruitful avenue of exploration.

While educated consent might represent an improvement in certain respects on informed consent, insofar as it puts greater stress on the communicative skills of the practitioner, perhaps 'valid consent' represents a better model than either 'informed' or 'educated' consent because they both erroneously imply that the possession of sufficient information is all that is needed to make a patient's consent valid. As Margaret McKeever's case, which we examined in the preceding chapter, forcefully highlights, information alone is not enough.

For a consent to be valid, there are three prerequisites: the patient must have received adequate information about the proposed treatment and its alternatives; no deception should have been used to obtain the consent; and the patient must be competent to consent to or refuse treatment. The term 'adequate information' is carefully chosen. There is no implication that the patient must know every single aspect of what is involved or every conceivable risk no matter how minuscule. It is the prerogative of the doctor to decide what the patient must know. Moreover, the doctor has the responsibility to ensure that a patient does not have unnecessary anxieties about treatment. Failure to meet any of these three conditions negates the possibility of a valid consent.

One model that has sought to respond to the importance of communication in the doctor-patient relationship is that of informed consent resulting from conversation. Just as the specific needs of an individual patient for information cannot be known by the doctor in advance, one cannot always predict how a conversation is going to turn out. One must follow the process along and respond to the cues from the unfolding conversation itself. This model has the advantage of implying that valid consent consists in a conversation designed to maximise patient participation in all health-care decisions to the extent that the patient seeks to be included.

The idea of consent resulting from conversation might, when properly developed, be a useful analytic tool for ethical issues of consent in medical practice and, more importantly and practically, could be a worthwhile educational device to highlight the skills and attitudes that a doctor requires to integrate into patient care. An important advantage of this model is that the patient is enabled to arrive at a better approach to health, e.g. the doctor may be one of the first to spot an eating disorder such as anorexia. A major problem in many such cases is that patients are not open about their problems. The conversation model helps the doctor to enable the patient to confront the problem and make an effective recovery. The difficulty with this model is essentially a legal one, since there is apparently an inherently subjective element to conversation that renders it inappropriate as a legal standard for review of controversial cases.

A conversation in which one is a participant is not the same thing as that conversation described to an outsider. A 'transparency model' is one way of overcoming this difficulty. In this model the key to reasonable disclosure is not existing standards of other doctors, nor a list of risks that a hypothetical reasonable patient would want to know. Instead, disclosure is adequate when the doctor's basic thinking has been made transparent to the patient. The patient is thus 'reasonably informed'. The doctor discloses the basis on which the proposed treatment, or alternative possible treatments, have been chosen and the patient is allowed to ask questions suggested by the disclosure of the doctor's information, and those questions are answered to the patient's satisfaction. The transparency standard requires the doctor to engage in the typical patient-management thought process, only to do it out loud in language intelligible to the patient. Both the conversation and transparency models are valuable since they stress the centrality of good communicative skills on the part of the doctor and in this way serve as a useful complement to the valid consent model.

Respect for patients' autonomy requires doctors to acquire and maintain skills in communication, not just informing, but also understanding. Doctors are faced with a double challenge: to develop their communicative skills and to retain their firm commitment to the welfare of the patient in the face of increased commercial pressures so as to empower patients, by enabling them to make informed choices. This is not to imply that doctors have to inform patients about every conceivable risk, however remote, in a particular course of treatment. As we have seen above, a 'fully informed choice' may not be possible because doctors could not be expected to communicate every possible risk to a patient nor could patients be expected to understand all the complexities of all possible treatments. Equally, a 'fully informed choice' may not be desirable for all patients because it might serve to generate unnecessary anxiety on the part of some patients if they were to be informed about every possible risk. Doctors need skills in communicating risks just as much as in understanding them. An example serves to illustrate the point.

Week One

A mother presents herself in Dr Fiona's surgery to confirm that she is pregnant. She is aged thirty-two and has one ten-month-old son who has been suffering from persistent chest infections. Dr Fiona has arranged for the child to have a sweat test. The results have just arrived and confirm her worst fears – the child has cystic fibrosis.

The other test shows that the mother is indeed pregnant. Dr Fiona has to break the news about her son. The mother is hysterical but nonetheless wants more information about her risk status.

Week Two

Dr Fiona asked the mother to return a week later to allow time to consult with her paediatrician. In her consultation she learns that the mother's risk status of having another affected child is one in four. Her husband has joined her for the consultation and while very keen to have more children he is reluctant to have another child 'if it turns out the same'. The woman is very upset and asks the doctor what are the risks for the child.

What is Dr Fiona to say to both? Medical care is based not on certainties but on probabilities. Every diagnosis involves an element of risk, i.e. the chance of an unfavourable outcome for a patient. An adequate understanding of risk is crucial to giving a valid consent, particularly as many medical treatments involve potent interventions whose side-effects are unlikely to be free from hazard. The explanation of risk also has major implications for litigation in medical care. Yet explaining risk is barely a Cinderella subject in medical ethics. It has not even got on the map.

The Long Arm of the Law

Two developments, in the medical and legal fields respectively, have brought the issue of consent to the forefront of debate in Western society. New medical treatments and technology are now capable of sustaining life in circumstances in which the social quality of the patient's existence is minimal or non-existent. On the legal side, a growing emphasis on the rights of the patient is emerging as a counterbalance to the traditional duty-driven principle of the sanctity of life. There are many thorny questions in this area. For example, the precise point at which society's interest in preserving life trumps the individual's right to autonomy is far from clear. Attaining a valid consent is not as easy as it might appear on the surface: there are difficulties both from a legal standpoint and from the practice of medicine itself.

In the case of Mrs Amy Sidaway in 1984, the British House of Lords rejected the 'American' legal doctrine of informed consent, which is based on patients' rights, in favour of a standard based on the obligations of the 'reasonable physician'. A further obstacle also in the British context is the belief that the financial consequences of informed consent would be disastrous. While in complete agreement with the belief that the collective health of the nation cannot be held hostage by a few who wish more expensive treatment, thus precipitating improper allocation of the community health-care resources, one must ask whether valid consent inevitably leads to this conclusion? While economic restrictions may prevent patient autonomy in every case, is it not possible for doctors to promote valid consent as far as is practicable and to the limits of what is allowed by their conscience?

On the other hand there is an impressive and steadily developing body of international case law that defines the doctor's obligation to patients in the area of consent. This area surfaced in Canada in 1980 in the case of *Reibl* v. *Hughes,* which stated that the law on capacity concerns 'the patient's ability to understand the information given and to decide rationally'.

The common-law approach holds, with only few exceptions, that medical treatment may not be given to an adult person of full capacity without his or her consent. In the United States the *Bouvia* v. *Superior Court* case affirmed a quadriplegic's right to have her feeding tube withdrawn even though she was not terminally ill. Likewise the case of *Lane* v. *Cardura* upheld the right of a competent individual to refuse amputation of a gangrenous leg, even though the procedure would have saved her life and she was otherwise in good health.

In *Miller* v. *Kennedy* in the Court of Appeals, State of Washington, it was stated:

> The duty of the doctor to inform the patient is a fiduciary duty. The patient is entitled to rely upon the physician to tell him what he needs to know about the condition of his own body. The patient has a right to chart his own destiny, and the doctor must supply the patient with the material facts the patient will need in order to intelligently chart that destiny with dignity.

The case of *Rogers* v. *Whitaker* in Australia in 1992 was noteworthy for its comments on the doctor's obligation in the area of provision of information:

> The law should recognise that a doctor has a duty to warn a patient of a material risk inherent in the proposed treatment; a

> risk is material if, in the circumstances of the particular case, a
> reasonable person in the patient's position, if warned of the risk
> would be likely to attach significance to it, or if the medical
> practitioner is or should reasonably be aware that the particular
> patient, if warned of the risk, would be likely to attach
> significance to it.

In the same year an even more forceful statement of patient autonomy
came in the *Re T* case.

> The patient's interest consists of his right to self-determination
> – his right to live his own life as he wishes even if it would
> damage his health or lead to his premature death. . . . It is well
> established that in the ultimate analysis the right of the
> individual is paramount. . . . The patient's right of choice exists
> whether the reasons for making that choice are rational,
> irrational, unknown or even non-existent. That his choice is
> contrary to what is to be expected of the vast majority of adults
> is only relevant if there are other reasons for doubting his
> capacity to decide.

The Right to Die?

The question of consent has been particularly prominent in cases
involving people at the end of life. In the case of Nancy Beth Cruzan,
the Supreme Court in Missouri were asked to declare a constitutional
right to die in 1988. She had lain in a persistent vegetative state
without hope of recovery since a car accident in January 1983, her life
maintained by artificial nutrition and hydration. Convinced their
daughter would not wish to continue to live in such a condition, her
parents sought to end her tube-feeding. Not only did the court say no,
they set a high standard of evidence for withdrawing treatment –
claiming that her guardians could not exercise her right to refuse
treatment for her and the State's 'unqualified' interest in preserving life
should prevail.

Two years later the case was considered by the US Supreme Court,
the first of many 'right to die' cases considered by State courts since

1976 to be heard in the Supreme Court. Ms Cruzan had indicated that she would not have wished to continue her life if she could not live 'halfway normally'. On a number of occasions she is reported to have said that if faced with life as a 'vegetable', she would not want to live. She also said, among other things, that 'death is sometimes not the worst situation you can be in' when compared to being 'sent to the point of death and then stabilised' without any reasonable possibility of 'ever really getting better'. While Ms Cruzan could not have foreseen her accident, were her statements not the best guide to her own wishes?

The 1988 Cruzan opinion was more than a failure to hear and obey Nancy Cruzan's voice. It was a refusal to let her next-of-kin speak for her. This made a nonsense of the whole concept of surrogate decision-making about life-sustaining treatment for a patient who could no longer decide for herself. Historically, both legally and medically, the convention has been to turn to the patients' families, to let them act as their agents, deciding as they would to the best of their abilities. The Cruzan verdict rejected this, stating that if there was a right to refuse treatment it was based on self-determination. The Cruzan verdict correctly stressed the gravity of a decision to forgo life-sustaining treatment. From that basis, the court concluded that this was not the sort of decision that can be ceded to a surrogate. However, the verdict apparently fails to consider that the decision to continue treatment is also of the utmost gravity – because it condemned Nancy to potentially decades of invasive treatment as she existed in a vegetative state. This, in turn, raises the question of whether the best interests of patients, families and society are served by raising issues of terminating life-sustaining treatment in a constitutional forum.

Closer to home in a landmark decision in 1995 the Supreme Court decided that doctors might cease feeding a woman who had been in a coma for over twenty years in a Dublin institution, thus allowing her to die. As a twenty-two-year-old she had suffered three cardiac arrests during a minor gynaecological operation, resulting in very serious brain damage. While the woman was not dependent upon an artificial respirator, she was assisted in feeding by a tube that was inserted into her stomach.

A major premise of Mrs Justice Denham's judgment in the case was that medical treatment may not be given to an adult person of full capacity without his or her consent save in exceptional cases, such as contagious diseases or medical emergencies where the patient is unable to communicate. According to the judge, the requirement of consent existed both at common law and under the Constitution; moreover, it was irrelevant whether the treatment was ordinary or extraordinary medical treatment or whether the illness was terminal or not. This premise emphasises the autonomy of the individual. The value of personal autonomy is further supported by reference to the constitutional rights to life in 'the recognition of the individual's autonomy, life is respected' – to privacy and to dignity.

> However we recognise that a competent adult may decide that they do not consent to medical treatment. The State's respect for the life of the person encompasses the right of the person to hold views such that for religious or other reasons they refuse medical treatment. In the acceptance of the person's decision, their life is respected.

The judge held that, irrespective of the ward's medical condition, she had a right of equality under the Constitution, which obliged the court to consider whether a method existed to give to the insentient person equal rights with those who are sentient. Among these rights were the right to life, the right to privacy – both of which, according to the judge, encompassed a right to die naturally and with minimum suffering – and the right to dignity.

Given the weight of legal opinion on the importance of consent, it is perhaps surprising that the Irish Medical Council in its *A Guide to Ethical Conduct and Behaviour* (1998) states that it would 'be reasonable to assume . . . tacit consent'. It would have possibly generated more public confidence if they had spoken of implied consent.

As in many other areas, there is a fine balance to be struck on the question of patient autonomy. On the one hand there was the case of Earle Spring, a seventy-eight-year-old man who suffered from senility and chronic kidney failure. As a result of his senility he was in a nursing home, and because of his chronic kidney failure he required dialysis. Although he had indicated to nurses that he did not want to die, his wife and son sought court approval to remove him from dialysis so that he could die. The Massachusetts Supreme Court approved this request – apparently on 'quality-of-life' considerations. This suggests that terms such as 'quality of life' are too loose and vague, too susceptible to corruption by judgements of social worth, and too easily directed against the senile and severely mentally disabled. It also suggests that autonomy for the vulnerable must be safeguarded.

One possible way forward that presents an obvious attraction is that decisions about the autonomy of the vulnerable should be grounded on the principle of 'the patient's best interests'. Such a shift does not end the problem, because clearly the criteria of 'the patient's best interests' are not evident. Efforts to provide more protection for incompetent patients by reducing discretion may well backfire if they are so restrictive as to simply swing the pendulum to the opposite extreme.

In November 1994 an English case highlighted the dangers of possible abuses of parents acting on a 'patient's best interests' rationale. A couple found guilty of manslaughter after refusing life-saving treatment for their nine-year-old diabetic daughter lost their appeals against conviction and sentence. Dwight Harris, a Rastafarian, 'clearly and deliberately' went against the advice of his GP and hospital doctors before 'emaciated' Nahkira died in hospital from a diabetic coma, said Lord Justice Kennedy in the Court of Appeal. He went on to add: 'Not only did he go against the advice, but in reality he must have watched that child waste – and society demands that an effective and indeed realistic sentence be passed against an appellant who behaves in that way'.

The court upheld the conviction and two-and-a-half-year prison sentence imposed on Harris at Nottingham Crown Court in November the previous year by Mr Justice Tucker, who had described him as a 'zealot' for refusing to allow hospital staff to give Nahkira insulin because of religious beliefs. Lord Kennedy ruled that the trial judge's summing-up to the jury had been 'impeccable' and the conviction could not be faulted. He also dismissed appeals by Harris's wife against her conviction and eighteen-month suspended sentence. The trial's judge said that she had been subject to her husband's stubborn will.

A particularly difficult area is when a Jehovah's Witness requires a blood transfusion. There is a further complication if that patient is a minor. Jehovah's Witnesses and other religious groups believe that there is a biblical mandate that firmly forbids spilling blood or making use of spilt blood. In the case of an adult Jehovah's Witness, blood may not be given against the patient's express wish, even if this failure results in the death of the patient. If we really accept the person's autonomy, we must respect her or his right to refuse consent, even when that competent decision is poles apart from that of the medical team, or appears to be idiosyncratic or even irrational.

In Ireland last year the parents of a seriously injured child refused on religious grounds to give consent for blood transfusion as part of surgical treatment. The practitioners involved brought the matter to the attention of the Gardaí, who invoked their powers under Section 12 of the Child Care Act. The child was treated fully for his condition, without the expressed consent of his parents. In effect, the local health board became his legal guardians for the purpose of granting consent to his life-saving treatment.

Last September Mr Justice Higgins ruled in the High Court in Belfast that a fifteen-year-old Jehovah's Witness should have a blood transfusion during a kidney transplant if necessary. The girl, identified as 'C', and her father, wanted the kidney transplant operation to go ahead but refused to give consent for a transfusion, while the mother, who is not a Jehovah's Witness, gave consent for both the operation and the transfusion.

It is surprising that in the US, where civil rights are so enshrined in the law, there still exists the conception of therapeutic privilege, which allows practitioners in some cases not to disclose to patients information that would prove harmful to them.

Capacity and Consent

To gain a better insight into the legal issues of capacity and consent I recruited expert advice in the form of Dr Deirdre Madden, Lecturer in Law at University College, Cork. In a lecture to the National Association of Mental Handicap in Ireland last year she elucidated some of the salient issues. There follows an abridged version of her lecture. Accordingly, the paragraphs I have selected do not necessarily follow on one from the other in her paper:

> The law relating to consent is of the utmost importance in medical law as it serves as means of protecting and preserving the right of the patient to decide what is to happen to him.[1] This is reflected in judicial statements to the same effect. For example, in the United States, Justice Cordozo stated: 'Every human being of adult years and sound mind has a right to determine what shall be done with his own body; and a surgeon who performs an operation without his patient's consent commits an assault, for which he is liable in damages'.[2]
>
> Also, in Australia, Brennan J. said: 'Human dignity is a value common to our municipal law and to international instruments relating to human rights. The law will protect equally the dignity of the hale and hearty and the dignity of the weak and lame; of the frail baby and of the frail aged; of the intellectually able and of the intellectually disabled. . . . Our law admits of no discrimination against the weak and disadvantaged in their human dignity. Intellectual disability justifies no impairment of human dignity, no invasion of the right to personal integrity'.[3]
>
> In assessing capacity to make health care decisions, what factors should be borne in mind by the clinician? A very interesting recent research project in the UK has demonstrated that for certain mentally incapacitated individuals, their capacity may be improved by use of simple language and non-verbal presentations.[4]
>
> To summarise the project very briefly may be useful: There were four groups of adult participants:
> 1. Those with mental illness (chronic schizophrenia or schizoaffective disorder).

2. Those with learning disability.
3. Those with dementia (Alzheimer's disease, vascular dementia or unspecified dementia).
4. Those with no mental disability.

All participants required blood tests either for general health purposes or to monitor medication levels and efficacy. Research involving the participation of those who may have been incapable of decision-making in such matters was justified by the relevant ethics committee on the basis that it would help to provide knowledge about the care and treatment of persons with their condition. It was also important that the research would not expose them to undue risk, it was not unduly invasive and it did not interfere with their freedom and privacy.

The research team developed information sheets which were written in simple language and in large font and comprised five elements:

1. The purpose of the law test.
2. The nature of the procedure.
3. The risk of saying 'yes'.
4. The risks of saying 'no'.
5. Voluntariness.

The outcome of the assessments based on a staged approach interview process was that 10% of those with a mental illness were found to be incapable of making the decision, 35% of those with learning disabilities, 67% of those with dementia and 0 in the group from the general population. The research team raised a number of points in their discussion of these results. . . .

- It is possible to improve an individual's ability to satisfy a capacity assessment if action is taken to work with them. The provision of information assisted some participants to move from being incapable to being capable. This is very important as developing a person's capacity gives due respect to their right to self-determination.
- Some participants were only able to move from being incapable to being capable when the non-verbal stage was

reached. This indicates that for some individuals alternative strategies for determining capacity ought to be adopted. The use of pictorial representations (preferably photographs as opposed to line drawings) which provide the necessary information element by element enabled a number of participants to move to being capable.

Twin Dilemmas

Few people could remain unmoved by the story of the Siamese twins known as Mary and Jodie. The twins were born on 8 August 2000 by Caesarean section at St Mary's Hospital in Manchester, with their bodies fused together at the base of their spines, their four legs splaying out sideways. They shared an aorta and a bladder, and their circulatory systems, muscles and skin were joined together.

Mary's heart quickly failed, as did her minuscule lungs, and consequently she used her sister as a life-support system. Hence Lord Justice Ward's rather emotive phrase in his judgment in the Court of Appeal: 'She sucks the lifeblood of Jodie, and her parasitic living will soon be the cause of Jodie ceasing to live'.

Jodie was a 'bright and alert baby'. Unless the twins were separated, Jodie would also die. Her parents insisted that the twins should not be divided and that both their children should be let die – a process that was estimated to take up to six months but, according to one of the doctors who examined them, might take years.

Their parents come from Gozo, a small island off the coast of Malta. Both are devout Catholics who rejected the opportunity to have an abortion after arriving in the United Kingdom. They said that they loved their daughters dearly and equally and were unable to contemplate the prospect of killing one to save the other. They were not optimistic about the sort of life Jodie could enjoy once separated from Mary. Lord Justice Ward in his judgment considered this opinion 'an unduly pessimistic view'.

The Court of Appeal's decision in the case was groundbreaking. It established that it was lawful to kill one innocent person – as distinct from simple withdrawal of medical treatment – in order to save another. Mary clearly had done nothing to justify killing her. This is the first time that the courts have sanctioned a treatment that is against the interests of a patient and inevitably would result in her death. Lord Justice Ward admitted that he had many sleepless nights over the stark question: 'Do we murder Mary to save Jodie?'

The judges in the case were at pains to point out the 'unique circumstances' of this case and that the ruling could never be used to justify euthanasia. Whatever result the courts came to in this case was bound to be unsatisfactory on some level, given the conflicting and irreconcilable considerations. Mary died the following November following the surgery.

One of the disturbing questions that the judgment raises is the question of the patient's autonomy – in this case, that of the parents who acted as guardians of the twins. Yet the parents' autonomy in this case was effectively ignored.

Given the intensity of the emotions that this case has generated on both sides of the argument it may be that in the immediate term we should focus on the incident as part of a wider trend. This case highlights that advances in medical technology are bringing us increasingly difficult, almost impossible choices.

It is difficult to set precedents that will have immense legal significance in this area. The question arises as to whether the law should have been involved at all.

To Legislate or Educate?
While the principle of consent needs to be unambigously enshrined in legislation, an excessively legalistic approach in this area may be counter-productive. Better education on the part of both the profession and the public may be more effective in the long term. In a pluralist culture the question is: whose morality, what law? Which principles should guide us in deciding which immortality should be described as illegal?

The Warnock Report on Human Fertilisation and Embryology represents a concerted attempt to define the moral role in liberal terms – attempting to legislate on the basis of a perceived implicit consensus. However, the Wolfenden Report on homosexuality and the Williams Report on pornography both abandoned the effort to establish a substantive consensus, opting for a course that made a distinction between two realms, i.e. a public realm, where ethics is enforced by a law, and a private sphere, within which individuals are left free to act on their own ethical preferences. A key function of a law is to protect the most vulnerable sections of the community, e.g. the severely disabled and the terminally ill – who might be threatened by prejudice. In Japan, for example, in 1987 there was a fundamental revision of legal procedures of the medical care and custody of mentally disordered people. This was a long overdue corrective to the 1950 Mental Health Law, which was enacted with the intent to protect society from the sinisterly termed 'harmful insane people' – which effectively deprived them of their fundamental human rights.

The Second Vatican Council's declaration of religious freedom put strong emphasis on the fact that nobody should be coerced to act against their conscience or be constrained from acting in accordance with their conscience 'within due limits'. In this context Patrick Hannon's use of the term 'due limits' in his masterly study *Church, State, Morality and Law* (1992) deserves special mention. He draws attention to the fact that the tendency to invoke this notion under the guise of the 'common good' is a denial of the major freedom that it confers. He correctly points to the fact that there must be a limit to the exercise of rights but insists that personal freedom is itself an intrinsic part of the common good; and care of the common good includes the promotion of all human rights. Thus recourse to the civil law simply to prevent the opening 'of the floodgates' is not desirable. It is up to a country's elected representatives and people to decide what kinds of laws the country needs. Morality cannot be legislated for. As Hannon has perceptively observed: 'In relation to morality the law's role is clumsy and humble. . . . It is wrong to expect too much of law . . . a propensity to legislate instead of to educate inhibits moral growth'.[5] No legislation, no matter how well it is constructed, can cover all the ethical ambiguities in life. To attempt to cater for every possible situation in the moral thicket would be a legal nightmare and inevitably would cause serious anomalies.

The human condition is dynamic and any ethical theory must be formulated with a concern for the particular as well as the general, which an absolute prohibition may deny. Such is the complexity of the human condition that ethical absolutes are difficult to sustain – unless they are thoughtfully and painstakingly nuanced and allow a legitimate place for exceptions.

As a layman I am tremendously impressed by the way the Dominican Order in its Constitution has always stressed the principle of 'dispensation'. Perhaps that is why the legitimacy of exceptions is recognised in the writings of Thomas Aquinas. Aquinas offers an important warning against an unbending moral legalism. He held that fairness or good sense, *Epikeia,* should be used to recognise when human law might be inappropriate in a particular case. In his words: 'Laws are made for human actions. But such actions are individual and concrete situations, and they are infinitely variable' and 'The law should not be followed when to do so would be wrong'. His theory of exceptions is in contrast to current unbending interpretations of his natural law. The application of *Epikeia* enhances justice, revealing glimpses of a higher 'law beyond the law'.

In this perspective, while we have, for example, an obligation to keep a promise, this obligation ceases if the keeping of this promise becomes impossible or immoral. Similarly, the obligation to secrecy is very important, but the grave needs of others or the common good might justify the revelation of a secret. While, as a norm, killing is wrong, not every killing is automatically wrong. Not every act of false speech is a lie. The more general ethical guidelines, such as the first principle enunciated by Aquinas – good is to be done and evil is to be avoided – are true in all cases. As we get into more specific situations, though, it is difficult to argue for absolutist positions.

In the course of the Falklands war a soldier was reported to have shot his trapped comrade in response to his comrade's anguished pleas that he was burning to death in a situation from which there was no possibility of saving him. Was that morally wrong? The duty to respect life may conflict with the obligation to minimise suffering and to respect autonomy. It is a cliché but a truism, nonetheless, that hard cases make for bad law. Good ethics depend on good facts. It may for example, therefore, be desirable to have a rule of practice that prohibits direct killing and authorises allowing some patients to die in some circumstances, even if this rule fails to fit every exceptional case that might be encountered or imagined. The function of reason in ethics is never simply to apply general principles to individual situations. The reality of the situation may not correspond to the ethical concept contained in the general principles, or to the common ethical terminology that expresses this concept, and so considers, for example, 'homicide' or 'theft' as unacceptable in all possible circumstances. Such terms are not merely descriptive, they are also evaluative.

For these reasons it may ultimately be more productive to educate rather than legislate for the practice of medicine. To do this task adequately will require us to answer a number of crucial questions. Is there a sufficient place for ethics on the curriculum of medical education? Do doctors in fact realise that care to nurture the patient's autonomy is as much part of medical practice as therapy and surgery? What about the patient? Does the educational system or the media ever really confront the issue of how 'lay people' should interact with doctors or with professional people in general? Education in this area might help remove some of the misunderstandings in the relationship between the lay person and professional, e.g. the patient (or client in the case of the legal profession) as powerless participant taking guidance without question from 'the expert'. Such an educational programme would require generosity and openness from the professions concerned. How willing have the profession(al)s been to subject themselves to outside scrutiny? Whose interests are served by the continuation of an asymmetrical relationship between the professional and lay person? Would not professional participation in educational programmes to empower the laity to participate fully in the doctor-patient relationship be an extension of doctors' commitment to service? Would not such an educational programme enhance the quality of the professional-client relationship and thus ultimately be to everybody's best long-term interests? The patient would be better informed and would be in a better position to develop a trusting relationship with the doctor. A complicating factor is that some patients do not always want to know the truth.

Nothing but the Truth?

In 1957 Dr Maurice Davidson began his chapter on truth-telling in a book on medical ethics with the following quotation from the book of Ecclesiastes: 'In much wisdom is much grief: and he that increaseth knowledge increaseth sorrow'. This highlights the human dilemmas doctors face in breaking distressing news to the already traumatised next-of-kin of patients.

Sissela Bok, in her book *Lying* (1978), considers three major arguments that are said to justify deception in health care in the context of fatal or grave disease, or in informing patients of the risks of treatment or research. Firstly, doctors' Hippocratic obligations to benefit and not harm their patients override any requirements of not deceiving people. On this line of reasoning, patients who are seriously ill already have sufficient problems, so why increase them by giving patients distressing news – particularly as patients' prospects of recovery often depend crucially on their morale? Passing on unpleasant medical information could possibly undermine these and consequently damage patients' prospects of recovery. Secondly, it is argued, with some justification, that doctors are rarely, or never, in a position to know the truth, since they can never be sure of the diagnosis or prognosis. Moreover, even if patients were told the truth, they would rarely, if ever, be in a position to understand it. Thirdly, it is sometimes claimed that patients do not wish to be told the truth when it is dire, particularly when they have a dangerous or fatal condition.

The principal problem with these approaches is that they show scant regard for patient autonomy – which forms a central part of the doctor-patient relationship. Deception in medical contexts almost certainly involves denying patients adequate information for rational deliberation. Even from a utilitarian viewpoint, it is reason to believe that in a particular case overall welfare would be enhanced by deception. The case of Breda Butler, which we considered in the preceding chapter, underlines the importance of this issue.

In this situation, the best judges of whether or not knowing the truth about difficult facts will or will not improve their welfare are the patients themselves. Clearly this poses a major practical problem: how can the physician discover a patient's opinions without disclosing any unpleasant facts to those patients who would prefer not to know such information? There is no easy answer. For some patients the most effective weapon may be denial. This may be established by sensitive questioning – a process that is very time-consuming for doctors.

Dr Pat O'Shea, in his Clint Eastwood-inspired title *A Fistful of Doctors* (1991), had some pertinent words of criticism for his colleagues in the medical profession:

> 'Hurry' is the commonest sin committed by modern general practitioners. Morning surgeries, afternoon surgeries, Saturday surgeries. For the patient, plenty of surgeries but very little time . . . . Patients pay for our expertise. Do they not also pay for our time?

The comments are addressed to GPs but they have a wider application in the medical profession – particularly in dealing with children and their parents. In the *Merchant of Venice* Shakespeare exhorted us to temper justice with mercy. Perhaps the lesson we can learn from the many anguished calls to radio phone-ins when the controversy about organ retention was at its peak is that truth-telling must be tempered with a measure of sensitivity. The experience of how Margaret McKeever heard that her daughter Sinéad had only six months to live, which we documented in the previous chapter, starkly highlights the need for this sea-change in medical practice.

A Modest Proposal

As we have seen, a new culture of 'transparency' is required whereby patients are provided with adequate information. However, information is not an end in itself. It is of little value unless it empowers patients to make good decisions.

One of the many interesting features of the Supreme Court's judgment about the woman in the so-called 'right to die' case we referred to earlier was Mrs Justice Denham's description of the communication between the medical profession and the family in the early stages of the tragedy as 'reminiscent of a Victorian era'. The other medical, ethical and legal issues have been trawled extensively. However, this aspect of the judgment has not received the attention nor the response it deserves.

Her comments highlight the desirability of inculcating a new culture of information provision and questioning into all health-service relationships. This, at a stroke, would transform the old paternalistic relationship between doctors who 'know best' and patients who are expected to accept passively what they are given. It would enable a decision-making process that is considerably better informed, at all levels, to come into being and allow for the use of the buzz phrase 'transparent'. A balance is required between potential good and potential harm. Often this balance can be difficult to summarise and explain to patients.

In the Irish context such communication problems are almost inevitable. The President of the Irish Medical Organisation, Dr Hugh Bredin, stated a few years ago that doctors are being forced to communicate with their patients at bedsides in obsolete, Victorian-style wards, within earshot of other patients. Moreover, due to lack of facilities, doctors often have to communicate with patients' relatives in corridors rather than in private rooms.

There are some hopeful signs. To take one example from the Irish context, the College of Surgeons is increasingly making both communication skills and medical ethics an integral part of its curriculum. However, as Professor George Silver of Yale University remarked in 1943, 'Medical education is a reflection of medical practice, it is not the education that will change the practitioners, but reformed practice that will redesign medical education.'

In this context it must also be stated that there is an urgent need to restrict excessive working periods for doctors. Apart from the consequent reduction in work efficiency, given the fatigue and lethargy that these draconian conditions induce, how can doctors provide the highest quality of personal care in these circumstances?

With a view to creating the maximum patient autonomy I would like to argue for the formulation of 'user-friendly' protocols, which would assist both patients and professionals to become partners in the information-exchange process. The protocols would outline some of the key questions patients would need to have answered before they could give a valid consent to treatment.

How would such protocols work in practice? An example best illustrates what I have in mind. Let us suppose a patient is seriously ill and the doctor suggests a new treatment of drugs, which carry the risk of side-effects. The protocol would outline the sort of questions that a patient would need to ask before consenting to this treatment. The questions could include the following:

- What are the likely side-effects?
- What are the possible side-effects?
- What is the prognosis without this treatment?
- What is this treatment designed to accomplish?
- Are there alternative treatments?
- If so, what are they?
- What treatment targets are to be pursued?
- In what circumstances would treatment be altered or stopped?
- How much research has been done on this drug?
- Would the physician use the same treatment on her/himself or loved ones?

Individual protocols would be drawn up for specific categories of patients, e.g. patients with genetic disorders such as cystic fibrosis; dental patients and dialysis patients.

To enhance the transparency process it would also be helpful if a 'health-care professional's contract' was debated and published, in which the health-care professional's obligations to patients, colleagues and society were clearly spelled out. This could well be in the professional's own interests, given the increase in litigation in health care. A significant statistic is that, according to a recent study, in 90 per cent of cases litigation in health care is ultimately caused by inadequacies in the doctors' communication rather than incompetence.

Ethics consultations, requested to help sort out what are deemed to be ethical problems in patient care, are becoming more prevalent. Conflicts may arise not only between doctors and patients but also among members of the health-care team when it comes to formulating and choosing goals of treatment. Such conflicts most commonly occur when

1. patients and doctors disagree on goals;
2. doctors and patients agree on the goals but the means necessary to procure such goals are ethically not acceptable to one of the parties;
3. doctors, family and members of the health-care team have different goals in view;
4. no clear goals have been decided upon;
5. the patient is incompetent to decide the goals of treatment, the patient has expressed no prior wishes and no clearly acceptable surrogates are known.

Ethics committees serve three valuable functions:

1. Helping to furnish options and formulating choices.
2. Bringing all interested parties into a dialogue.
3. Decreasing the frequent feelings of powerlessness and guilt that all concerned have when dealing with issues in which no ideal solution is available.

Ethics committees cannot resolve every conflict because ethics is ultimately a matter for individual agents; the key question remains: What am I supposed to do?

It may be that a court of law is not the best forum to resolve this issue because of a lack of specific medical expertise. Perhaps the creation of some kind of national mediation service comprising legal and medical expertise and patients' representatives could be piloted. For the sake of the reputation of medicine it is important not only that justice should be done but that it should be seen to be done.

I would also like to suggest that independent ethics appeal boards might be established on a trial basis – whereby patients could have their grievances dealt with in a much less combative and expensive forum than the courts. The appeals board would be comprised of a broad range of representation, with medical, legal and ethical expertise and patients' representatives. The verdict would be binding on both sides. However, the priority ought to be to ensure that cases do not need to go to arbitration in the first place. Better communication between doctors and patients would go a long way towards achieving this.

Notes

1. Kennedy and Grubb, *Medical Law, Text with Materials* (London 1994), p. 87.
2. Schloendoff v. Society of New York Hospital, 211 NY 125 (1914).
3. Department of Health v. JWB and SMB, 66 ALJR 300 (1992) pp. 317-18.
4. Gunn, Wong, Clare, Holland, 'Decision-Making Capacity' *Medical Law Review* 7 (Autumn 1999), pp. 269-306.
5. Patrick Hannon, 'Abortion dilemmas', *Tablet* (14 May 1992), p. 39.

3

WHAT'S UP, DOC?

On 2 May 2000 a tribunal under its sole member, Judge Alison Lindsay, began investigating how contaminated blood products were administered to haemophiliacs in Ireland in the late 1970s and 1980s. These imported blood products did initially bring significant improvements to the lives of people with the condition but it also gave them HIV and hepatitis C. As a result of using products supplied to them to treat their haemophilia, over a hundred people in the State became infected with HIV and approximately two hundred became infected with hepatitis C. Some were infected with both. The tribunal came too late for seventy-four haemophiliacs who had already died because of their infections.

The tribunal was spawned by the hepatitis C tribunal in 1997, which investigated the infection of pregnant women with the Anti-D vaccine. The Irish Haemophilia Society had unsuccessfully sought full legal representation at the tribunal. It withdrew its participation in January 1997 on the grounds that its terms were too restrictive. The Government finally agreed to establish the Lindsay tribunal to consider the infection of blood products with HIV and hepatitis C. It was not plain sailing all the way because the Irish Haemophilia Society had to face down the Minister for Health and force him to yield to its demands for guarantees that its costs for taking part in the tribunal would be covered. Mr Martin Hayden, counsel for the Irish Haemophilia Society, addressing an early hearing of the Haemophilia Infection Inquiry, incisively observed: 'This is not an inquiry into brown bags to politicians, or rezoning. This is people's lives, their deaths and the effects on their families'.

In the dock on a variety of fronts was the Irish Blood Transfusion Service (previously the Blood Transfusion Service Board) under examination for the criteria it applied to donor selection, screening and testing, the treatment of blood products and the board's decision-making procedures, for example: had the BTSB a policy or guidelines to ensure its products were as safe as possible? Why was unscreened plasma used in BTSB products? However, the spotlight was also on the Department of Health in terms of the effectiveness and appropriateness of its response to the infections. Another agency under investigation was the National Drugs Advisory Board, which licenses such products. Indeed, the fundamental question must be posed: why do we need a tribunal to establish how and why these crucial matters of life and death went so wrong?

On the opening day of the tribunal, counsel for the tribunal, Mr John Finlay SC, spoke of the great courage of victims who were volunteering to give evidence in coming forward to describe matters that were 'obviously deeply hurtful, private and sensitive'. He expressed the hope that one of the benefits of the tribunal would be to dispel some of the ignorance and prejudice that surrounds the conditions of HIV, hepatitis C and haemophilia. Special arrangements were put in place to preserve the anonymity of infected persons who gave evidence, including the erection of a screen from behind which they could give evidence. Some victims and their relatives availed of the opportunity to relate their stories and articulate their grievances without any such restrictions.

One such person was twenty-year-old Karen Stephens, who was the first witness to give evidence to the tribunal. She courageously waived her right to anonymity to tell of the effect on her life of her father's infection from contaminated blood products. His lungs failed and his spine collapsed from bone disease. Jerome Stephens died in August 1993, just before her thirteenth birthday.

> I never had a childhood. Parents of children attending my school told their children not to touch me and if they did they ran to wash their hands. People called me names and spat at me.
>
> What I really want is my dad back, but that's not going to happen. There isn't a night that I don't think of him and cry. It seems so senseless. I want to know why he was taken away, why he's not going to be at my wedding.

In many cases the tribunal has held up a mirror, not only to the medical profession but to some of the dark corners of Irish society. We can only wince at the prejudice we see in the reflection. Mr Raymond Kelly, whose teenage son John died of AIDS in 1994, recalled how John suffered from haemophilia and was given a contaminated clotting agent in 1984. A year later he was diagnosed HIV positive. John never, to the day he died, knew that he had HIV. His family constantly had a finger on the button of the remote control on the television in case a news item would come up that would link haemophilia with HIV and AIDS.

Mr Kelly found it difficult to find a school for John. The headmaster at the first school he approached said he would have to tell all teachers in the school that John was HIV positive. He also tried an 'upmarket' private school, where the principal said all teachers and their wives would have to be told.

In May 1994 John had a severe stroke. His speech went, his eyesight was going, he was screaming, and his father brought him to hospital. The medical personnel said they could not do anything for him and asked Mr Kelly to take John home. John died three months later.

Mr Kelly raised some of the wider issues that the tribunal needed to address.

> I want answers to questions. I know what I think happened. He was infected by products brought into this country from America. I want to know who brought them in, who made the decisions and if they knew they were contaminated or possibly contaminated, which I think they did. If they did, then they murdered my son.

The distressing narratives of anguish and agony furnished the proceedings with a human context in preparation for the more technical element of the hearings. One of the most important findings to emerge early in the tribunal was that one of the board's own products, Pelican House-made factor 9, caused haemophilia B patients to be infected with HIV in 1985 and 1986 – but those infected were not informed. This immediately highlights the ethical issues that are raised by this sad chapter of Irish medical history. However, as we will see from the following cases, there are wider issues raised about the doctor-patient relationship.

Agatha's story
A health-care professional took the pseudonym of 'Agatha' at the Lindsay Tribunal and her late husband was referred to during the course of her testimony as 'Ronald'. Ronald acquired both the HIV virus and hepatitis C.

> Haemophilia is a blood disorder and it's carried by females and it's transmitted to males and there's haemophilia A and haemophilia type B. Haemophilia is a factor VIII deficiency and haemophilia B is a factor IX deficiency.
>
> I first met my husband in July 1981. He was tested in January 1985 and he was informed in August 1985 that he was HIV positive.
>
> We married in August 1987. I became pregnant. I did appreciate the risks but I was very confident that I was going to be all right. I suppose if I wasn't, I wouldn't have survived. When I was seven months' pregnant, Margaret King in the Irish Haemophilia Society organised for me to have a test done; she said it was best to wait until I was seven months' pregnant, and I had the test done and I was negative. So I didn't inform the consultant whom I was attending in the maternity hospital because I didn't feel it was any of his business and I would have known the staff in the maternity hospital as well and I just felt if I was negative I wasn't putting anybody at risk so I didn't want anybody to know my business. My husband was so private about it and so anxious about the whole lot he didn't want anybody to know either. My son was born but he never was tested because unless I was positive, he's not positive.
>
> In 1991 Ronald was diagnosed as being hepatitis C positive as well. In 1993 he was commenced on Interferon, which is an injection that he took subcutaneously on a daily basis. He was

on that treatment for six months. He suffered with fatigue and his appetite wasn't great as a result of being on it, so following six months of treatment he decided he would just discontinue it because he felt that he had no quality of life. The treatment was part of a trial.

In November 1994 Ronald was diagnosed as having CMV of his eye and he was admitted to the hospital from 29 November to 9 December. He had to have a port cat put in underneath his skin here and he had to have treatment twice daily, but he was very depressed in the hospital so the doctor said that he could go home and I (as a health-care professional) was able to give him the treatment at home. So on 9 December he came home to me.

On 16 December he was readmitted. We went in at 10.00 a.m. and we had to wait until after 4.00 p.m. in the evening for him to be admitted because there was no beds. He died on the twenty-first.

I seek that the full extent of everything that occurred to be out in the open; about the treatment, about the fact that treatment was imported here and it was banned in America. For two years after it was banned in America, it was still being administered to the haemophiliacs here. Somebody had to have known, somebody isn't letting on or else their eyes were closed to what was going on, it didn't suit them to know, I don't know. And also, for my son's sake, that when he's old enough to know what the circumstances are, that I can give him the full facts, not just half the facts, all the facts. And for Ronald's parents as well, that this can be all put to bed. I mean, I don't expect that parents believe that they should bury their offspring before they die themselves. This has taken a toll on a desperate amount of families and even when the tribunal is over, they still have to pick up the pieces.

Everybody should be treated the way you would like to be treated yourself, and maybe everybody should look at the situations like that. They should have been properly informed, properly counselled, and there should have been facilities put in place that would have cushioned an awful lot of the suffering that all of these people have experienced. I mean, these boys were people's fathers, brothers, uncles, parents, there's no end to the amount of people that have suffered.

A Father's Love

The pseudonym 'Peter' was used by one of the witnesses at the Lindsay Tribunal who spoke of his own experiences and his family's experiences in relation to his late son, who was discussed using the pseudonym 'Dermot' – in terms of Dermot's infection, HIV and his subsequent death. Dermot was born in 1957, the second of a family of seven and died when he was thirty-nine.

> When he was a week old, on his christening day, he became very ill and had to be taken to the hospital and he was subsequently diagnosed as being haemophiliac. It was very severe. He was a Haemophilia A, which is the Factor VIII. If he had a knock . . . it was hospitalisation immediately for transfusions to alleviate the swelling and the pain.
>
> As we moved into the '60s there was a change in the available treatment. It was still a transfusion. I don't know if it was whole blood or an extract. I think it was an extract of blood because progress had been made, quite a lot of progress had been made in treatment at that time. This was cryoprecipitate and he was on it on up into the '70s. We always felt that progress was being made and we hoped that progress would continue, that things would get better. And I suppose to an extent they did. And then things got very, very much worse.
>
> As he grew up he suffered from internal bleeding. He had difficulty with his joints in later life and couldn't walk properly. He didn't start school until he was somewhere between six and seven years old. He always had problems with his joints, his knees, his elbows, if he got a knock, of which he got plenty.
>
> The factor could be used immediately, in the home if he got a knock or a bruise. He could go and take it straight away and it would prevent the swelling and the pain coming up. That was

a great advancement. He administered it himself and because of the speed with which he could get the treatment, it stopped any great swellings.

In 1984 or 1985 his hip gave him terrible trouble and he had a hip replacement, but that hip replacement subsequently had to be removed – about nine years later. It gave him terrible trouble in the end, with infections, one thing and another.

I believe that my son had been told sometime in the '80s that he had contracted an infection, but he didn't tell us immediately, he didn't tell us for quite a long time. So we, his family, did not know for definite that he had contracted an infectious disease. But he did eventually tell us – probably in the early 1990s. It was an occasion when he had been in hospital and one of my daughters was coming down for the week and she brought him home with her. And they came into the house and my daughter said, 'Dermot has something to tell you' . . . actually it was she who said the words that my son had an infection, had been infected with hepatitis.

It's very hard to describe feelings; devastation, because it was like being given a life sentence. What we understood was that his problem was a disease that was eventually going to take his life. And it did.

He was still being treated in hospital on a regular basis but neither he nor my family were offered counselling. These were harrowing times. They still are.

The last three weeks of my son's life he had been in hospital and he was feeling pretty sick. And we went up there one day and we came into the haemophilia ward and it was there that he was told that he was dying. There was nobody with him when he was told. It caused a lot of distress to his mother and I, that he should be told in those circumstances. It shouldn't have happened. I thought it very insensitive, very cruel. We came in after he had been told. He was shocked. He couldn't even speak. He was very, very angry.

Afterwards when we came in, we spoke with the same doctor and he told us. He said that our son's illness was now so severe that he was going to die and there was nothing anymore that anyone could do for him, and that he had a life expectancy of about three months. He told us that his liver was packed up and could no longer function, was no longer functioning – which meant hepatitis.

When the doctor had left the office – he only spoke to us for a few minutes – there was a nurse there, and she made us a cup of tea, talked to us. She said his life expectancy was nearer to three weeks than to three months. She said she didn't think he would live three months, and he didn't, he lived three weeks.

We were told that there was nothing more that could be done for him. He wanted to come home, we wanted him home. We dressed him – the first time in his life he ever let anyone help him dress, got him in a wheelchair, brought him down the lift in a wheelchair, out to the car, and we brought him home. During those three weeks we had no contact with anyone except the members of the Haemophilia Society. No one contacted us, called us or came near us other than that. For most of the last week of his life he slept a good deal and he just passed off in his sleep.

For something like that to happen shows an awful lack of care on somebody's part. It shows utter carelessness or incompetence. My son did not commit suicide, he did not die of natural causes. He was killed. He was killed just as if someone had walked up to him, put a gun to his head and pulled the trigger. For all the unfortunate people who died, I'm thinking of them as well. I only hope that this tribunal is going to first of all find the truth of what happened, why it happened and who was at fault.

I think that there is a terrible dragging of feet on somebody's part, because I'm sure that the contamination was known of long before it was made public. With haemophiliacs, they are a very vulnerable section of our society because they are so dependent on blood products to alleviate pain and suffering. They were let down. They were let down very, very badly by those in power and those in authority and those charged with seeing that all those products were right, screening and testing. They were let down.

The product was brought in from the United States. When a donation of blood is made by a donor in Ireland it's completely free and voluntary, but in America they get paid for donating blood, and any Tom, Dick and Harry could walk in off the streets in the United States of America and donate blood and get paid for it. It shouldn't have been sought there, I believe. The risk of infection from blood imported from places like America are greater than Irish blood. But then there was probably a consideration, financial consideration, and it all boils down to money, doesn't it?

Dignity in Death?

Another witness gave testimony to the tribunal using the assumed name of 'Larry'. He spoke about the life and death of his father-in-law.

I knew him from the time I started dating my wife at the age of sixteen in the early '70s. I knew then he suffered from haemophilia. We got married in '83 and I lived with him up to his death.

Around September of 1984 he came up to Dublin for a prostrate gland operation and we were told around that time he would have to have the spleen removed as well. The day after the operation he was very well, and was sitting up in the bed when we came to see him. He was in great form. He received treatment for his haemophilia in conjunction with the operation.

I'd say about a week later a doctor told us that, while he was improving, they didn't think he was doing as well as he should be and he was a bit depressed and they thought he would do better at home. Now, he didn't want to come home and we didn't want to bring him home because we didn't think he was well enough to come home.

When he came home he wasn't very well. He couldn't heal. He wasn't eating anything and his stomach was swelling. He had a follow-up appointment for the next week and he turned very yellow and jaundiced, like, every bit of him was yellow, and we brought him back for the follow-up to a specialist, and himself and his wife were brought in to him, and the specialist told him he was doing fine and that he was to be seen in three months' time. He was so weak that I was practically afraid to bring him to Dublin that day for his appointment, I thought he wouldn't make it, but we had to bring him back home that evening.

He was very tired and very ill. We thought he shouldn't have been at home. Then one Saturday night in November myself and my wife were away and we got a phone call around half six in the morning to say that he had taken a turn at home, he had haemorrhaged blood, and that a neighbour had brought him to the local general hospital.

He went in on a Sunday morning and we asked for him to be sent to Dublin because we felt that they couldn't cope with what he had. They said they didn't think there was anything that could be done in Dublin that they couldn't do, but he had told me himself they were trying to get some blood for him and they weren't able to get blood. So we came on to him about getting back to Dublin and I think it was the next day they sent him to Dublin.

When he returned he was very ill and, shortly after, he went unconscious. We were never told what was wrong, we were just told that he was very ill, and we already knew that. We stayed with him for a couple of nights and days and some of the staff informed us, like, that maybe it would be good to go home and get a rest and if there was any immediate change they would contact us. We went home on a Thursday evening. On the Friday morning around 3.30 they rang a neighbour's house to say that he had taken a bad turn but we weren't to rush up the road, and they rang back in a half hour to say that he had passed away. The hospital rang on that morning to see could they do a post-mortem, and we agreed. Now, we don't know whether it was ever done or not, we never got any report from it.

We made arrangements for the funeral. We headed up on that Friday, approximately 3.30, to the hospital mortuary, and I was met at the mortuary door by the undertaker, a local man, a friend of mine, and he told me that he had been informed by the staff that nobody was to touch the body and that there were two security guards; one at one side of the coffin and one at the other side of the door to see that no one touched the body.

As people arrived I had to meet them at the door because, approximately fifty or sixty people came to accompany the father-in-law back to his home place. And we had to tell them not to touch the body.

I don't know how they took it but we didn't take it very well. We thought we should have been informed before, as we felt that if we had known, we would have had it privately at a funeral home and avoided that particular embarrassing situation.

While we were in the mortuary, a doctor or nurse came to me and asked me had his wife been sleeping with him. And I said she had. She said she should not have been sleeping with him. I didn't ask her why at the time, as you can understand, it was in the mortuary and the funeral was about to leave. But she did instruct me that she would give me plastic gloves and plastic bags to dispose of all his belongings, such as razor or anything like that. I was told to burn them and I did, without even thinking. I did not ask why at the time. This all happened, like, while we were in the mortuary, you know, so it was sort of sprung on us.

There were some kind of plastic gloves or something on his hands and that's about all we could see, top of his hands and top of his face. I didn't have any views at the time because it was all sprung on us so quickly, everything happened at the one time. We think now we were treated very badly on it and that we should have been prepared better on the day. We think at least we should have been contacted by someone in the hospital and they, not the undertaker, should have told us not to touch the body.

My wife read an article in the paper a day or two after where a man died in the hospital from AIDS and we presumed it was her father, we always thought that.

At the time we were unaware of any communication between personnel from the hospital and the BTSB concerning blood products. No one ever discussed that type of correspondence with us.

We applied for the death certificate for his wife to get his pension, and it took us a long time to get it, it took nearly a month to get, and in the long term we had to drive to Dublin to obtain the certificate. The cause of his death put on it was 'Hepatitis' and I think 'four days' was written on it.

It's had a big effect on my wife, who's had to have counselling over the years for it. She was an only child and very attached to him and she has had to have counselling even up to no later than six months ago, and the counsellor told her it was all related to her father's death. She's very depressed.

There's a lot of unanswered questions for which we'd like to just get the truth. We were never told anything, we had a right to be told.

Accidental Disclosure

One mother used the pseudonym 'Felicity' to tell her story at the tribunal. She has three sons. All three have hepatitis – having contracted it from contaminated blood products. In 1995 she discovered by accident from a nurse at a hospital that all three had hepatitis. Felicity believes that if she had realised one son was infected, she might have been able to save the other two.

I have three children with severe haemophilia B. Two were admitted to hospital for investigations into severe bruising in 1985. There was a question mark over child abuse but they were diagnosed Factor IX deficiency, which would call for all this fair bruising. The bad news was that haemophilia was a lifelong condition and the good news was that the concentrates they had now to treat haemophilia would mean they would lead a perfectly normal, healthy life. I had another son born in 1987 and he was diagnosed with haemophilia at six weeks.

My husband brought up the thing about AIDS, the AIDS tragedy that had been earlier on that year, and we were assured that the factor was gone and that this wouldn't happen again.

In 1988 or 1989 one of the children went on prophylactic treatment – preventive treatment, which means you treat it in advance of a bleed. You'd be given treatment twice a week, which would eliminate any joint damage.

When people started to die from hepatitis C there was no need to ask the doctors as to whether my children had hepatitis C because all these people were much, much older and nobody told me different.

My youngest son is a very happy-go-lucky type child. He's quite content in himself. He loves sport. He's a happy person who's quite healthy. He was fine until, in late '95, this all changed. While he still seemed to be quite healthy, he became very depressed, withdrawn, suffered huge bouts of fatigue, crying for no reason. So straight away I suspected maybe he was being bullied in school. I went down to the school and exhausted all the avenues and there was nothing there. So I decided to ring the hospital. I rang and spoke to a nurse and said I was very concerned about him, he was very depressed, he had no energy, and I thought he was suffering from depression, and I asked her did she think it was possible for a child so young to suffer from depression.

She said, 'No. Maybe it's his hepatitis.'

I said, 'He doesn't have hepatitis.'

The nurse said she would go away and check the list. She said, 'all three of your names are on here'.

I thought she made a mistake. I panicked. I rang the Irish Haemophilia Society. I don't know what I said, but still, in the back of my mind I kept thinking she's after making a mistake.

There are seven people living in my house. We are on home treatment, which means that while they would be very careful with needles, there is always the risk of an accident or if one of them is bleeding.

That's unforgivable, because for the five years that they left me wandering around in the wilderness happy as Larry, they should have been at least registered with the hepatology clinic, so that would have meant for five years their livers were untreated, unmanaged, they could have died. And I wouldn't have known why. I'm very angry. I can't understand why I wasn't told. Maybe they never wanted to tell me.

They were diagnosed in 1990, but altogether, the three of them were diagnosed on different occasions. If somebody, somebody had checked those results, the other two could have escaped. If they'd have thrown away the factor and brought in the other stuff, all three of them should have escaped. But two, definitely. I was assured that this wouldn't happen again. That the factor was – state of the art factor. The other stuff was gone and it wouldn't happen again. I was assured that nothing like the AIDS thing would happen again. And then we turn and we have hepatitis C. It didn't happen in other countries. Why did it happen here?

It's very bleak for my children. They won't reach their full educational potential. They're going to miss a lot of the time from school, which means they won't achieve as much as they could do. The concentration is gone at times. They suffer with fatigue. I'm afraid that they'll throw in the towel before they even start.

It's something that you don't tell somebody, as there's a lot of social stigma to it. They would wish, this might sound funny, but they wish they had cancer instead because you can tell people you have cancer, you can't tell people you have hepatitis C. And if anybody finds out, that's it, they won't be your friend anymore. For a relationship, it would take a very special girl to be told that her prospective partner has hepatitis C. Would you like your daughter to marry somebody with hepatitis C, no matter how they got it?

After being told that the AIDS thing wouldn't happen again and then hepatitis C happens, I often wonder what else is next?

Is there anything else in there? Who can we trust? I trusted them. They told me that was safe. I gave that to them. I feel responsible for this, but I'm not responsible. Somebody else is responsible for cutting corners. That stuff wasn't treated properly. It didn't happen in other countries. Nobody learned anything from the AIDS thing. Because straight after that it was soon forgotten about and they went on to hepatitis C. So I don't think anybody learned anything. It was the same old story, forget about the small haemophilia community, maybe they'll all just die and go away.

I want the tribunal to find out for me why I was left for five years not knowing that my children were infected but while putting their health even at further risk and my family. I want to know what I'm going to tell my children when they ask me who's responsible. I hope that my children do not end up with Hepatitis C because somebody was trying to save money.

Ambushed

On 4 May 2000 a father of five, Bernard Smullen from Newbridge, County Kildare, became the first infected person to speak at the haemophilia tribunal without any restrictions being placed on his identity.

I received the Factor 8 clotting agent after I was injured in a road traffic accident in 1980. I was diagnosed with hepatitis in the same year but did not know what type.

I found out I had hepatitis C in 1993. The previous year I had a bleed and went for treatment. One of the sisters asked me if I wouldn't mind speaking with Dr Anne Tobin who was doing research in St James's Hospital into hepatitis at the time. As much out of a curiosity as anything else I went to see her. I had a number of scans and initially they were inconclusive. Then it emerged that I had some liver damage. The testing procedures in Ireland at the time were not as sophisticated as they are today, so my samples had to be sent to America. The result was that it took over a year from my first meeting with Dr Tobin before I was finally diagnosed as having hepatitis C.

I don't know if the consequences were ever fully discussed with me other than that we should take certain precautions in our intimate life and with toothbrushes.

Because of the infection I lived with depression for many years, as a result of which some of my children became alienated from me. I had become contrary and difficult to live with at home. My family had become worried about my state of mind. My troubled state of mind was one the symptoms of the infection, but all those years I didn't know for a long time exactly what they were symptoms of.

When I found out the reason for my behaviour was hepatitis C it was a relief. However, the initial diagnosis came as a shock. Originally, when I escaped the HIV virus, I felt relieved. When I discovered I had hepatitis C it was like being ambushed.

My brother is haemophiliac and has hepatitis C. As a consequence of his illness, he had to sell his business, he had a nervous breakdown and continues to receive psychiatric treatment. My fear is that it will affect me in the same way.

I have constant fears about other infections I might pick up when I get treatment for a bleed. They tell us now the treatment is synthetically produced, but nobody knows. The incubation period for CJD was believed to be up to twenty years. So how do we know there will be no more viruses?

The infection has resulted in me being passed over for promotion and I live in constant fear that my condition will deteriorate.

I am employed by the Turf Club and it would be expected I would socialise with people I did business with but I was unable to do so.

Prior to the diagnosis I had enjoyed sport. I was secretary and chairman of a soccer club in Newbridge but had to resign in 1989 as it became too much for me.

I continued to see a psychologist and was worried about my wife becoming infected.

I believe somebody knew I had hepatitis C going back to the early 1980s but I had to find out about it by a coincidence – when by accident almost I came into contact with Dr Tobin.

I have had a lot of experience with the medical profession since childhood because of my hemophilia. Doctors spoke about your condition to colleagues in front of you but they didn't speak to you.

I remember once when I was in my early teens I had a bleed in my hip and I was in the Richmond Hospital. A consultant came along one day and brought his entire class of medical students to my bedside and without asking me if I would mind or anything he launched into a full examination of me, with the class using me as a guinea pig almost. It is not the sort of experience that enhances your self-worth or sense of human dignity.

In fairness, in the last few years I have noticed that doctors are changing. In the past doctors didn't speak with you, they spoke at you. If I was in hospital and a new doctor was examining me for the first time he would just take my file and without asking me anything he would launch into his view of all that was wrong with me without giving me the opportunity to say anything about how I felt. Nowadays that doesn't happen as much. Doctors today will start by asking you how you are feeling.

There is still room for improvement. The one change I would like to see doctors making is to realise that we are living in an era of instant communication and that patients shouldn't have to go to third parties to find out all the details of their condition. Doctors have got to be up front with patients.

I do think the State needs to get its act together when it comes to its role in health care. I am not just talking about haemophiliacs here but about the community generally. We have a two-tier health system. I am lucky enough to be able to afford to join the VHI so I know I will not be on waiting lists for eighteen months. Other people are not so lucky.

Six years ago my mother died. She was left on a trolley in a hospital from eleven o'clock in the morning until six in the evening, even though she was in great pain and distress, because wards in the hospital were shut down. That kind of thing

shouldn't happen. People shouldn't have to spend their final
hours of life in those conditions. Nobody should have to suffer
like that. What's the point, for example, in the Government
building a new hospital in Tallaght if they are not able to open
up all the wards or resource them?

The lesson that the State needs to learn is that you can't put
a price on people's health.

For Your Eyes and Ears Only?

As these often shocking testimonies clearly illuminate, there are many
difficult questions to be answered. The problems are compounded by
the fact that two of the key principals in the BTSB are missing from
the Lindsay Tribunal, having died subsequently. One of them had
shredded key documents, including the dockets that could have
identified which product and which company had been responsible
for infecting haemophiliacs. The dockets would have allowed the
people infected to take legal action against the companies. One of the
principals seems to have been involved in a serious conflict of interest
because of his commercial activities outside the BTSB.

As all the personal testimonies clearly indicate, victims feel that
they should have been given specific information by the medical
professionals but were the medical professionals precluded from
revealing such details on the basis of patient confidentiality?

Historically, confidentiality has been considered a cornerstone of
the doctor-patient relationship. The seminal work on the duties of the
physician to the patient, the Hippocratic Oath, stated: 'And
whatsoever I shall see or hear in the course of my profession, as well as
outside my profession in my intercourse with men, if it should be what
should not be published abroad, I will never divulge, holding such
things to be holy secrets'.

Such has been the gravity attached to confidentiality in the doctor-
patient relationship that it has in the past often been erroneously
compared to the seal of the confessional. However, confidentiality is
not an absolute in health care. There are four legitimate exceptions
when a doctor can break confidentiality:

ITEMS ON ISSUE
FOR Mr James Clinch
ON 23/12/09 18.40.20

BX001614039006
Dexter Colin
Morse's greatest mystery and other stor
Issued 09/12/09 19:49:05
Renewed 23/12/09 18.39:58
    Count 1 (1 unseen)
Due 23/01/10

00917964669006
Rendell Ruth
End in tears
Issued 23/12/09 18:40:11
Due 23/01/10

18539058289003
Scally John
Doctor's orders
Issued 23/12/09 18:40:07
Due 23/01/10

1. When a court directs the doctor to so do.
2. When the patient has explicitly consented to disclosure.
3. To prevent the patient from causing harm to others or society at large.
4. To prevent patients from doing harm to themselves, e.g. in the case of a severely depressed patient who may be on the brink of committing suicide.

Much more problematic is when doctors are confronted with a conflict situation whereby both breaching and maintaining confidentiality bring inherent risks. This is best illustrated by an example.

A thirty-four-year-old married man is referred to a doctor because of a three month history of diarrhoea associated with a two-stone loss of weight. Whilst abroad on a business trip six months prior to the onset of his current symptoms he had a sexual liaison with a woman. The patient is now HIV positive. He does not want his wife to know the diagnosis or of his affair. His twenty-seven-year-old wife wants to know what the doctor's investigations have revealed. In a previous consultation she has expressed the desire to start a family. How is the doctor to handle this situation?

Failure to respect the confidentiality of medical records represents a serious breach of the patient's right to confidentiality, while silence exposes the wife to potential infection. In such a situation how can this conflict between the rights of the patient and the welfare of his wife be reconciled? Instinctively we would all wish to ensure that partners in these situations would not be put at risk of infection. However, if a doctor does breach confidentiality in these circumstances it is almost inevitable that this patient will lose confidence not only in that doctor but in all health-care professionals. More alarmingly, if it emerges that doctors are breaking the confidence of patients who have the HIV virus, people with the virus or people who are worried that they may have the virus may not wish to come forward, thus exposing themselves and others to further risk. Inevitably, this will diminish the therapeutic relationship. However, confidentiality can not be used to justify preventing patients or their guardians from receiving relevant information about their health.

There was an allegation early on in the tribunal that a patient's condition had been openly discussed in front of other patients waiting to be seen at a particular hospital. This raises important questions about how seriously some professionals take patient confidentiality.

Sense and Sensitivity

The testimonies we have considered chronicle a series of incidents that provide a damning indictment of the medical profession and the wider management of the health-care system. Unfortunately the Lindsay Tribunal is not a new story. The Finlay Tribunal investigated how hundreds of women had been contaminated with hepatitis C. Who will ever forget the harrowing details of the Brigid McCole case?

Important questions to be addressed by the Lindsay Tribunal are: How could haemophiliacs continue to be infected with HIV despite the availability of treatment to deactivate the virus in blood products? What were the interrelationships between hospitals, the blood bank and the Department of Health as the catalogue of deaths mounted?

While the chilling chain of events that caused dozens of haemophiliacs to lose their lives are best investigated by the Lindsay tribunal, I wish to deal with the wider issues in the doctor-patient relationship raised by the controversy. As we have seen, a recurring theme of the personal testimonies given by victims or their relatives in the tribunal was a frustration at a lack of knowledge over what caused the infection and, more particularly, their feeling that some shadowy figure had taken the decision that the victims should never know. This again raises major questions about consent, which we considered in the previous chapter.

There are many other questions. How could Felicity be allowed to hear about her sons' infection in such a shocking manner? How could Bernard Smullen have his humanity so diminished when he was treated as a human guinea pig? How could Larry's father-in-law be treated with such a lack of dignity in death? How could Larry's family be treated with such insensitivity? How could any health-care professional ask if a wife, numbed with grief, had been sleeping with her husband as he lay just a foot away in a mortuary?

The testimonies we have examined offer merely a snapshot of some of the problems in the doctor-patient relationship. There were many other disturbing claims, including the allegation that one doctor yawned immediately after informing a patient that he had hepatitis. These stories underline the need for a detailed examination of the doctor-patient relationship. A consideration of the various issues involved constitutes my task in the next chapter.

4

TRUST ME, I'M A DOCTOR

My Doctor's Face

A face at peace
Or covered with anxieties,
All animation dulled from overwork;
A face which gives me meaning
with its welcome;
Or shuts me out with quiet disapproval;
A face so tense and hurried
That you feel
His worries must be many more than mine.
What is that face
which stays so calm and listens,
so competently examines, treats and reassures?
May it be that face
I shall be meeting
which gives me the will and strength to live once more.
(Author unknown)

The word 'trust' is sometimes used in an ironic way, e.g. Joseph Heller's character Slocum in *Something Happened* describes another character: 'He knows I drink and lie and whore around a lot, and he therefore feels that he can trust me'. However, in relation to health care, from the earliest of times trust includes the expectation that doctors will respect certain ethical limits.

It is difficult, if not impossible, to attempt an exhaustive survey of the history of medical ethics because of the lack of material available on this area from the ancient period. While fresh archaeological evidence brings new information, there are still large gaps in our knowledge. In 1901 a French archaeological expedition uncovered a copy of the legal code of Hammurabi, the sixth king of the First Dynasty of Babylon, who ruled from c.1790 to 1750 BC. Of the 282 laws, nine pertained to medical practice. These laws reflect the stratified paternalistic society in which they were conceived. They were an attempt to regulate 'medical practice' in an era when medicine was necessarily rudimentary in the absence of sophisticated technical expertise.

A more developed statement of the medical and ethical care required on the part of professionals was to emerge with the 'Hippocratic Oath', an effort to outline some of the duties of the physician in the fourth century BC. The text of the Oath was as follows:

> I swear by Apollo Physician, by Asclepius, by Health, by Panacea and by all the gods and goddesses, making them my witnesses, that I will carry out, according to my ability and judgment, this oath and this indenture. To hold my teacher in this art equal to my own parents; to make him partner in my livelihood, when he is in need of money to share mine with him, to consider his family as my own brother, and to teach them this art, if they want to learn it, without fee or indenture, to impart precept, oral instruction, and all other instruction to my own sons, the sons of my teacher, and to indentured pupils who have taken the physician's oath but to nobody else. I will use treatment to help the sick according to my ability and judgment, but never with a view to injury and wrong-doing. Neither will I administer a poison to anybody when asked to do so, nor will I suggest such a course. Similarly I will not give a woman a pessary to cause abortion. But I will keep pure and holy both my life and my art. I will not use the knife, not even, verily, on sufferers, but I will give place to such as are craftsmen therein. Into whatsoever houses I enter, I will enter to help the sick, and I will abstain from all intentional wrongdoing and harm, especially from abusing the bodies of man or woman, bond or free. And whatsoever I shall see or hear in the course of my profession, as well as outside my profession in my intercourse with men, if it

be what should not be published abroad, I will never divulge, holding such things to be holy secrets. Now if I carry out this oath, and break it not, may I gain forever a reputation among all men for my life and for my art; but if I transgress it and forswear myself, may the opposite befall me.

In the Middle Ages comparatively little was written about medical ethics, and ethical theory was in the main rudimentary. An example that may serve to illustrate this was John Arderne's *A Treatise on the Fistula*. The preface of this book offers an account of the rules of professional etiquette and ethics. The 'leech' (an archaic term for a physician) is advised not to be boastful or rash in speech or action, not to deprecate colleagues, not to ogle fair women in great houses, not to be overbold in prognosis and not to undercharge for services. A young physician was also advised to learn a few good proverbs, which were to be used to comfort patients.

From the outset the medical profession has never been shy about the claims it made for its members. In ancient Greece the good physician was a gentleman with a love of wisdom and a commitment to a life of virtue. The third-century BC author of the Hippocratic text 'On Decorum' claimed:

> For a physician who is a lover of wisdom is the equal of a god. Between wisdom and medicine there is no gulf fixed; in fact medicine possesses all the qualities that make for wisdom. It has disinterestedness, shamefastness, modesty, reserve, sound opinion, judgment, quiet, pugnacity, purity, sententious speech, knowledge of the things good and necessary for life, selling of that which cleanses, freedom from superstition, pre-excellence divine. What they have, they have in opposition to intemperance, vulgarity, greed, concupiscence, robbery, shamelessness.[1]

Six centuries later the physician was described in the *Hymn of Serapion* to the God Asclepius in the following way: 'He would be like God, saviour equally of slaves, of paupers, of rich men, of princes'.

With the speed of technological advances the medical profession has indeed acquired God-like powers. However, it is unlikely that the public will be quite as deferential to the medical profession as these early authors envisaged. Even in classical Greek times, the man who worked for money by selling his services on the open market was frequently despised. Plato, for example, had little respect for physicians who saw medicine simply as a means to secure a good livelihood. The physician in Chaucer's *Canterbury Tales* provides a good example of this trend: 'gold in physik is a cordial therefore he loved gold in the special'. The sociologist Geoffry Hurd claims that a significant minority of doctors today see medicine simply as, 'the gateway to the good life'. The United Nations Declaration on Human Rights, however, recognises that every person has the right to a decent livelihood, including doctors. Invariably opinions as to what constitutes a 'decent livelihood' will differ greatly. Is self-interest the dominant factor in the professional–client relationship? George Bernard Shaw encapsulates the view that self-interest is the main motivating force of professionals in his comment that: 'All professions are conspiracies against the public'.

In reaction to the medical profession's 'self-image of benevolent caretaker', Ivan Illich describes the medical profession as a 'radical monopoly' in which 'the social control of the population by the medical system' becomes a 'principled economic activity'. Illich claims from his study of underdeveloped countries, that the professions are responsible for elitism and for the creation of dependency on the part of the clients.[2]

The fact that all is not well in the doctor-patient relationship is indicated by the significant increase in litigation in medicine.

Legal Eagles

Writing about changing patterns of medicine in Ireland and specifically about the increase in litigation, Dolores Dooley observes:

> Medical litigation in Ireland is primarily a painful symptom of patients' frustration in their efforts to get answers to questions asked, whether about diagnosis, choice of therapy, or prognosis.

The lay public feel impotent when confronted by the enormous imbalance of power among professionals, hospital institutions and patients.[3]

She goes on to suggest that litigation occurs partly because doctors and patients are 'as strangers' to each other: specialists often do not know their patients before they perform radical surgery on them; strangers are more likely to sue each other because they have no 'shared context of trust'.

The threat of malpractice litigation casts a shadow over medical practice and places a great emotional strain on doctors and a major financial burden in the form of higher insurance premiums. While patients should be appropriately compensated in the event of injury or harm during the course of medical treatment, excessive litigation undermines the very fabric of such treatment. Patients too have obligations to the doctor, as they are both partners in a reciprocal relationship; these obligations must include justice, and justice must determine when patients have recourse to the courts. Perhaps the present climate of litigation is yet a further sign of the need for a much greater level of professional–client education so that patients can fully understand the dynamics of their interaction with the doctor. The reality of medical practice, for example, includes the possibility of making non-negligent mistakes or of experiencing 'bad outcomes' even without making mistakes, hence the distinction between medical misadventure and medical negligence.

So how then should we consider the relationship between doctor and patient from an ethical point of view? Sociologists like Zbigniev Brezinski argue that in the post-industrial society, knowledge and its communication will replace economic ownership as the main source of power. According to this approach, since professsionals have knowledge and therefore power, they have the burden of discerning how this power is to be used in a responsible way, hence a greater need for questions of professional ethics. Is this additional power to be used to achieve greater social conformity and dependency on the professionals, or to open the system to wider and more authentic participation by all? Working from the same premise of the post-industrial society, another strand of sociological opinion represented by Alain Touraine in his book *The Post-Industrial Society* suggests that a new characteristic of the professions today is their de-personalisation. Accordingly, the major new ethical questions for doctors are: how do they use their technological mastery for the service of humankind and how do the doctors enable patients to transcend the de-personalisation of technological systems?

In the Line of Duty

Moral responsibility centres on providing an account of the rightness and wrongness of our conduct in the service of the self and service to the other. The basis of this account is found in our ability to reason together in a careful, precise and rational fashion about the person's moral obligation or duties or character. The former concerns what one ought or ought not to do when confronted with a particular situation. The latter concerns what sort of person one ought to become, so that one not only acts rightly but is also a good, morally praiseworthy person.

A number of approaches to duty are possible, one of the most famous of which is Immanuel Kant's idea of the 'categorical imperative', i.e. 'Act only according to that maxim by which you can at the same time will that it should become a universal law'. Kant argued that each rational being has a worth and a dignity apart from any end to which she or he might serve as a means. In the Kantian scheme, rational beings invariably treat other rational beings the way they would like to be treated themselves, since to do otherwise involves inconsistency, and to be inconsistent is anathema to rational beings. When we interact with other rational beings we are compelled to consider their worth as individuals. By treating them as a means (however good), we use them only for some purpose, thus shattering their right to be treated as an end. As we have already seen, however, patients, in a variety of situations, have been treated as means not ends. People are an end in themselves, not a means, and ought never to be modified, or fabricated, simply to serve an ulterior purpose.

Bedside Manners

It is possible to view the relationship between the doctor and patient in a number of ways. In one presentation the necessary characteristics of professional caring include elements that are affective, cognitive, volitional, motivational, imaginative and expressive:

Dr A cares professionally only if A:
1. experiences positive regard for the person being cared for (affection).
2. intellectually grasps what is essential to the well-being of the person cared for (cognition).
3. commits expertise and energy to secure the well-being of the person cared for (volition).
4. is emphatically able to enter and share in the world of the one cared for (imagination).
5. is moved to care primarily because of the commitment to secure the well-being of the person cared for (motivation).
6. demonstrates caring behaviours that are perceived as such by the one cared for (expression).

Carl Rogers in his book *A Way of Being* (1980) identified three ways of counselling that he had established – genuineness, unconditional positive regard and empathy. A person is genuine when what they think and say is the same thing. Unconditional positive regard means that the other person's humanity is valued without qualification. It is not just aspects of a person that are deemed as good, but all of the person matters. Empathy is understanding and appreciating the feelings of another person and being able to communicate this to the other person. Essentially this means that health-care professionals must accept other people as they are, and be with them as they are themselves. It also means interacting and being open to what the practitioners may meet, and meeting it without judgement or assumptions. The value of this insight for medical practice is to highlight that there can be a profoundly ethical dimension to the way the health-care professional asks, 'How you are you feeling today?'

Thus before the medical profession comes to the 'problems', before one acts at all, there is the question of a fundamental disposition, a disposition to respect the other, to do her or him good. All the qualities associated with such a disposition, such as patience, kindness, compassion and reverence, are not extraneous accretions but key elements in what the ethicist Pedro Lain Entralgo calls 'the medical friendship', the delicate alliance that simultaneously nurtures confidence and discourages dependency, and are as much part of the doctor's ethical behaviour as is the ability to discern what is to be done in difficult situations.

The medical profession has from the outset recognised the need to ensure that its members do not exploit their power over their patients. Now the medical profession is very clear that there are four key ethical principles that should animate the doctor-patient relationship, i.e.

1. First do no harm.
2. Do Good.
3. Autonomy.
4. Justice.

The key to the moral component of the profession is the concept of 'doing good' for the client. The professional assumes the duty of promoting good for the client in the area of avowed expertise. This concept of promoting good is generally specified as the moral principle of beneficence; a firm commitment to benefit the client. The principle of beneficence can be considered as involving a continuum of actions; at one level 'do not cause evil or harm' (nonmaleficence), extending through the prevention of evil or harm, the removal of evil or harm, and finally, the highest conception of beneficence, doing or promoting good. An immediate problem presents itself: whose conception of the good should predominate – the professional's or the client's?

Other professions too have dilemmas in this area. In an article in the *Guardian* in 1991 a lawyer spoke as follows:

> I remember a custody case for a most disagreeable man whose wife had left him with the children. I remember reducing her to

floods of tears in the witness box and I felt very badly about it because I thought she was a nice woman, which she was, and her husband was a shit. On professional grounds I knew I had done a really good job. But as a father of young children I really thought that the right result hadn't been achieved.

An additional moral obligation on the professional is to weigh possible benefits against possible harms, to maximise benefits and minimise risks of harm. Utility requires that the professional achieve the greatest value of benefit (value) over harm (disvalue). This introduces a further consideration, the professional's obligation to respect the autonomy of the client, i.e. to allow the client to participate in the decision-making process that will result in the professional dealing with the client for her or his benefit, which we have already considered in our discussion of consent.

As we have seen, traditionally it has been advocated that the principles of beneficence, autonomy and justice represent the basis of a good relationship between the professional and patient. However, the codes of the medical profession appear to distort the balance by over-emphasising beneficence and relegating autonomy to a secondary, even peripheral position. Unless the commitment to benefit the patient is complemented by an equal commitment to nurture the patient's capacity for self-determination, in the area of health care, the medical profession runs the risk of paternalism. The good of the patient might simply become what the doctor decides, rather than what the patient in close consultation with the doctor decides.

Traditionally, the health-care professional–client relationship has been structured around the concept of what can be termed the 'clinical model', which is utilitarian and teleological (end-centred) in its interpretation of the relationship. The patient is considered to have a disease produced by either an external factor or a malfunctioning structure, which is the source of pain and discontent. Effective management (through good treatment) is the aim of the physician, which, if successful, will restore the patient's well-being. The relationship between health-care professional and patient is one where the controlling expert relates to the patient as an object to be carefully observed, evaluated and expediently dealt with by effecting a 'cure'. The relationship is teleological insofar as the role of the physician is that of a provider of good consequences and her or his actions are good to the extent that they bring about ultimate happiness, i.e. in this case, relieve pain and suffering. This gives the impression of the powerful physician, who through his or her skill and expertise acts upon the more passive patient, who co-operates obediently and thereby is restored to health.

A superficial analysis might easily elicit assent to this approach, since the primary motivation is to work for an alleviation of pain and misery. However, a British National Ambulatory Medical Care Survey revealed that in addition to technical medical skills needed by the family physician, in family practice the physician is often called upon to relate to a patient whose complaints appropriately lie outside the boundaries of the 'clinical model' and pertain instead to the 'affective state'. Pain is a dual phenomenon, firstly the perception of the sensation and secondly the patient's psychological reaction to it. A person's pain threshold varies according to mood and morale. Fear, anger, sadness and depression lower the pain threshold. However, sympathy and understanding can raise the pain threshold.

The 'relational model' focuses on the quality of the process of health-care professional–client interaction rather than on the successful management of the case. By stressing the quality of the process, the relational model is compatible with the position of Immanuel Kant. In this approach, certain attributes of acts themselves are judged to be inherently good over and above any results that may ensue. Consequently, an act may be right even if it fails to produce beneficial consequences. Kant argued that each rational being has a worth and a dignity apart from any end to which she or he might serve as a means. What are the implications of this philosophical approach for doctors in treating their patients?

In this perspective the patient has a need to be cared for and the doctor responds to this need with 'care' in the broadest sense. The nature of this care shifts focus to that of process rather than product, 'care' rather than 'cure', and away from a narrow teleological relationship to one between doctor and patient as persons, both of whom possess equal inherent value. Literature has something to contribute at this point, because it offers a vivid way of expressing concepts such as the understanding of the patient as person, with which we may be familiar in the abstract. Solzhenitsyn captures the spirit of this relationship:

> No doctor likes filling up forms, but she put up with it because for those three months they became her patients, not pale mergings of light and shade on a screen but her own permanent living charges who trusted her and waited on the encouragement of her voice and the comfort of her glance.

The crucial insight of the 'relational approach' is that it gives adequate attention to the absolute value of both doctor and patient as persons who have mutual obligations of respect for each other, neither using the other as a means. However, the 'relational approach' does not conflict with the teleological approach, as both approaches complement each other: the teleological focus ensures that the 'medical problem' is confronted, while the relational focus protects the 'patient in pain' as a person during the course of treatment.

Conflict

Few people would disagree with the four principles we have identified that are intended to animate the doctor-patient relationship. What could be more clearcut? The only problem is, what do they mean? Let's take a case. Suppose we have a person who is at the end of their life, with a terminal illness and in great pain. I am the doctor and I want to reduce the person's pain and I know that I can immediately prescribe drugs that will reduce that pain but will equally reduce the patient's lucidity and capacity for autonomous judgements and also hasten their death. What does 'do no harm' or 'do good' mean in this situation? The principles are very clear – what is not so clear is how to apply the principles in specific situations. In medical ethics, decisions about right and wrong will seldom present themselves in black and white but more probably in bewildering shades of grey.

As if applying the four principles was not complicated enough – what happens when there is a conflict between two or more of the principles? Some years ago there was a famous case in England of a man who was a repeated sex offender, who asked that he would be surgically castrated. The doctors said no – that this was a violation of the 'do no harm' principle as it represented an attempt to find a physiological solution to a psychological/psychiatric problem and that the same result could be achieved by drugs. The man insisted that under the principle of autonomy he was entitled to make the decision. The court found that there was not a genuine informed consent because the man was not willing to listen to the alternatives.

This case is interesting on many levels – not least of which is that the final decision was made in the courts. Increasingly complex medical ethics decisions are no longer made at the patient's bedside but in the courts. It also highlights that autonomy is not an end in itself.

Another source of complication for medical ethics is the speed of technological advances. Technology has put new and impressive means at our disposal that have rapidly changed our assumptions and our expectations concerning the management of illness and life. Vital organs are replaceable, emerging life can be scanned for defect, death may be postponed until another time. But pressing problems do not wait for answers. 'What are we to do?' quickly becomes 'What ought we to have done?'

Playing God

The two great constants of human existence – birth and death – were for centuries a matter for God and nature only. Now science has intervened. The news that a fifty-nine-year-old woman gave birth to twins on Christmas Day 1993 and the suggestion within a fortnight that eggs from aborted foetuses be used to restore the ovarian function in sterile women to create babies prompted a tidal wave of comment – some of it illuminating, much of it not. The ghost of Frankenstein was regularly invoked and terms like 'womb-robbing' were bandied about with wanton abandon.

On 5 October 1992, Marion Ploch, a young German woman on her way home from work, drove her car into a tree, smashing her skull.

Ms Ploch was flown to hospital and put on life support. Doctors found that she was brain dead, but when they sought permission from her parents for organ donation it was refused. After three days she showed no reflexes whatsover and was entirely dependent upon a lung machine, along with an IV, for fluids, nutrients and medication. She was pronounced dead on 8 October. Her foetus, though, estimated to be four months old, was not dead but alive and still growing. What catapulted the case to international notoriety was the doctors' decision to keep the mother's body actively functioning until the foetus would be viable, approximately seventeen weeks from the time of the accident – a time span that would have surpassed all other similar attempts, if the treatment had been successful. The extended use of existing medical technology, which enabled the surgeons at the Erlangen University Medical Clinic to keep her body animated until the following year, when they hoped to deliver the child by Caesarean section, brought the medical profession into unchartered waters.

Nobody knew who the father was, and he never came forward. The woman's parents agreed to this suggestion, although they later claimed that they consented only under pressure from doctors. On 16 November the foetus spontaneously aborted and died. Sections of the German media criticised the doctors' actions, seeing them as a grisly experiment that destroyed the dignity of the woman's death, and called for tighter controls over clinical practice. The case raises many difficult ethical questions. While this situation was exceptional, the technology involved was not, so has the realm of medical practice been radically extended? Has it even been redefined? Does this exceptional case take us one step closer to what one day may be routine treatment? At what cost: financial, medical or ethical? Are new ethical coordinates now needed?

Down through history a number of methods have been employed to 'ensure' that a baby would be born of a particular sex. In ancient Greece, tying of the left testicle was said to do the job, while medieval husbands drank wine and lion's blood before copulating under a full moon. Other methods include mating only in a north wind or hanging one's underpants on the right side of the bed. Since 1993 a 'designer baby' service in a London gender clinic is available, where couples who are desperate to have a baby of a particular sex can receive 'assistance' – although there is not a 100 per cent guarantee that the outcome will be a baby of the sex they choose. This development raises serious questions about the manipulation of sex and brings the process of childbearing, to some extent at least, into the area of quality control. The clinic has imposed restrictions to the treatment; for example, they do not make their services available to a couple who already have a boy and a girl, or have none at all, and are not party to abortions if the sex selection process is not a success.

In October 1993 an American fertility expert, Dr Jerry Hall, announced at a scientific meeting in Montreal that he had cloned human embryos. Splitting embryos, as Hall had accomplished, uncovered a technique that could give doctors the ability to produce identical twins, and possibly triplets or quadruplets or even more, to order. There was also speculation that one might keep a spare copy of oneself in deep freeze, to be grown to maturity later so that its organs might be 'cannibalised' as the need arose: new parts for old, and a perfect genetic match to ensure compatibility. Hall justified his discovery on the grounds that it could be helpful to infertile couples, by increasing the number of laboratory-fertilised embryos available for transfer into the womb. As less than one in ten of such embryos 'take', a stock of spares could increase the success rate for pregnancies.

Cases such as these have generated a lot of public anxiety that medical science has gone too far and that humankind has taken on powers hitherto reserved for God. Contemporary society has witnessed suffucient evidence of the destructive and dehumanising potency of scientific experimentation and achievement to view it with some caution.

The twenty-first century has already been labelled the 'biotech century'. Throughout its history humankind has shown a remarkable capacity to adjust to change. What was extraordinary rapidly becomes ordinary with the pace of scientific and technological advances. As a race we have benefited enormously from these advances. At the same time we recall that there have sometimes been major discrepancies between the promises of the scientific community and subsequent developments. Who will ever forget the shambles of the BSE crisis?

How are we to shield ourselves from the excesses of technical advances in medicine while preserving the benefits of modern health care? How can we ensure that our knowledge and our needs remain in step? How are we to keep science from encroaching on our rights and dignity while nurturing basic values and ethical principles?

Never before have the possibilities open to humankind been so great, and yet hand in hand with these exciting developments in science and health care a certain fear has taken root, a fear of what might be called the dehumanisation of medicine.

Since the birth on 25 July 1978 of Louise Brown, the world's first 'test tube baby', the technology of IVF and related procedures, for example, has repeatedly thrown up ethical dilemmas, while legal and ethical guidelines have trailed behind. In the early 1980s the Warnock Committee attempted to grapple with the questions and agreed a wide-ranging set of recommendations, but it was not until the Human Fertilisation and Embryology Act of 1990 came into force that these recommendations were passed into law. The controversies did not go away, particularly relating to the use of IVF for single women and lesbian couples.

In March 1991 further controversy was created over 'virgin births' when it emerged that the British Pregnancy Advisory Service had accepted for counselling three women who had never had sex but wanted children through donor insemination. The answers have not come as fast as the questions.

A consequence of the increasing technology is that the traditional ethical question has been turned on its head. Historically, ethicists have asked the question: how can people be brought to do what they ought? Today, increasingly ethicists are asking: when should people be restrained from doing all that they are capable of?

A recent case that raised this question was that of Adam Nash. Adam was born in Englewood, Colorado on 29 August 2000 after being genetically screened as an embryo before being implanted in his mother's womb in an effort to save the life of his seriously ill sister. The embryos, provided by the children's parents, Lisa and Jack Nash, were screened to ensure the best possible transplant match for Molly. On 26 September, life-saving stem cells taken from Adam's umbilical cord were transplanted into Molly as a treatment for a rare inherited disorder, i.e. Franconi anaemia, a bone-marrow disease. As a result Molly was said to have up to a 90 per cent chance of being largely free of the condition. Some commentators claimed that an unacceptable ethical boundary had been crossed and alleged that it was the first step to choosing the right-coloured eyes and the right intelligence.

New technology holds out the prospect of great medical advances but also the danger that the patient as a person will recede into the background and that the relationship between the sick and those who care for them will be violated.

Ambrose Pare (1510–1590), a noted French surgeon, said that doctors should comfort always, alleviate often and cure sometimes. This insight needs to be recaptured today.

If something becomes technically possible, is it therefore ethically responsible? In many cases the answer is yes. At other times, however, the answer must be no because a particular technique is found to be against human dignity and at variance with the true purpose of medicine itself, i.e. a service to the human person as a whole. What has happened is not so much that the scientists and medical personnel involved have been unconcerned about whether or not they were making responsible use of their knowledge and skill. The problem is that mutually inconsistent forms of ethical evaluation have come into play, but this inconsistency and the inadequacy of some of the approaches have not being recognised.

What is urgently required is an approach to ethical questions in this area that will allow us to reason through the problems that arise on the basis of an appreciation of what makes life human; how real human values can be enhanced or jeopardised; how human dignity and rights are nurtured, and how they are assaulted. This approach will consider such principles as free and informed consent; respect for human dignity at all stages of life; adequate previous experimentation, and sufficient benefits to justify the risk of failure. Above all it demands that the professionals involved and all interested parties should come together to formulate a blueprint of how medical progress can be compatible with the understanding of a vision of the meaning and purpose of human life. Advances in medicine, a bit like Celine Dion's heart, will go on and on. In the interim, ethical assessments will, therefore, tend to be tentative, cautious and provisional as further progress is made and refinements of technique emerge.

Medical dilemmas are bewildering because doctors and families want to act in the best interests of patients but are unsure about the scope and content of the obligation to care. An adequate ethical framework in relation to the treatment of terminally ill patients, for example, is not just a mere individualistic situation ethic, one that points to the uniqueness of each case, but one in which the norms inform the situation, and vice versa, the situation determines the norms. Such an ethic provides basic convictions, basic attitudes, motivations and norms. What is required is a standpoint, an orientation, a coordinating system, a compass. A new attitude to treatment is a further consequence of the respect due to every human being. It is not just a matter of treating illness, a disease, but of seeing the people who are ill, and of recognising that every form of care for human life is meaningful.

In Alexander Solzhenitsyn's powerful novel *Cancer Ward*, one of the patients, Pavel Nikolayeich, makes a heartfelt complaint: 'This impersonal treatment, it's terrible'. This observation articulates the feeling that it is an assault on a patient's dignity to be treated merely as an object of health care. The patient ought to be approached as a whole person, taking due account of her or his emotional, social, religious and communicative conditions. Doctors are participant observers in the problems confronting their patients because it is their function not only to alleviate symptoms of pain, including disabling anxiety and depression, but also to safeguard the dignity, responsibility and respect of the patient.

The health-care professional's job, which connects daily with the pains and fears of others, carries with it commitments not common to most other jobs, or, at least, not to the same degree. Patients, by virtue of their increased vulnerability, must entrust a greater part of themselves to the goodwill of their doctors. They hope, justifiably, for a response to that trust that treats them with human concern and respect, as well as with professional knowledge and skill. As a norm they are not disappointed in that hope. The danger is that as technique becomes ever more dominant, the human face of health care might become obscured. Patients come to surgeries with apprehensions and particular expectations. When these patients are treated as persons, their fears are allayed and the expectations are met with excellent care, empathetic treatment, and with continuing good health.

Time To Say Goodbye?

Perhaps after 2400 years it is time to say goodbye to the paternalistic beneficence of doctors and to the principles of Hippocratic ethics. The principles espoused in the Hippocratic Oath are particularly unfit to support the recognition of a patient's self-determination as an integral part of her or his individual civil rights.

Medical ethics will have to change from paternalism to partnership. The expectations and aspirations of society in relation to professional services generally have changed significantly over the last fifteen years or so. A better educated public is increasingly conscious of its rights and, encouraged by consumer organisations and the press, expects and is able to demand a high standard of service. Legislation, too, places an increasing duty on the professional person to ensure that his or her work and activity are beyond reproach. In the medical context, patients are far more aware than they were in the past and are prepared to make an effort to find the latest treatment and to obtain the information on available services. They are also more prepared to complain if they are dissatisfied with the results. The profession must respond positively to these shifts in public attitude by enhancing the services it provides and the manner in which they are provided.

Only by maintaining the highest standards of behaviour towards patients, colleagues and the public will the trust of the public and the profession's privileged position, which results from this trust, be retained. What is required is a consideration of the values and principles that animate professionals' intuitive judgements, that bring them into contact with problem cases and then move to achieve some degree of consistency. In this debate the public's voice must be heard because we cannot let the ethical questions in medicine be settled by default.

While the recent scandals illustrate the urgency of a far-reaching review of the doctor-patient relationship, they also illuminate the need for a fundamental review of the way the medical profession regulates its members and deals with the public. It is to these issues that I now turn.

Notes

1. Hippocrates, 'Precepts VI', in *Hippocrates 1*, trans. W.H.S. Jones, (Cambridge, MA: Harvard University Press, 1959), p. 319.
2. Ivan Illich, *Medical Nemesis: The Expropriation of Health* (New York: Pantheon, 1976), p. 94.
3. Dolores Dooley, 'The 1980s: A Decade of Change', *Hastings Centre Report* (Jan–Feb 1991), p. 21.

5

WHO WATCHES THE WATCHERS?

The doctor gets you when you're born,
The preacher when you marry.
The lawyer lurks with costly clerks
When too much on you carry.
Professional men they have no cares,
Whatever happens, they get theirs.

Ogden Nash's cynical comments clearly illuminate the power of the professions. The medical profession has manifestly huge power in the Irish health-care system. This state of affairs brings the potential for abuse. We are not born ethical beings. We become so through a conscious choice. As recent Irish history has demonstrated, in a wide range of activities some people take the road less travelled when it comes to ethics.

In June 2000 the Irish media reported that two Irish health boards had been forced to order a total review of 2000 diagnoses undertaken since 1991 by British pathologist Dr James Elwood, at three hospitals in Kerry, Donegal and Sligo. The review came as it was claimed that one Kerry cancer patient was diagnosed by Dr Elwood as having a completely different type of cancer to that from which she was actually suffering. Dr Elwood was already seventy years of age when he first arrived at Tralee Hospital for roster relief duties in January 1991 after he went into semi-retirement from his position at the Princess Margaret Hospital in Swindon.

Immediately the Minister for Health, Micheál Martin, announced that he would be reviewing medical monitoring and certification following the revelations. In media interviews the minister admitted it was 'absolutely extraordinary' that no upper age limit exists for practising clinicians. Public anxiety about the case was accentuated by the fact that the media reports also claimed that Dr Elwood was the focus of a major probe into serious mistakes involving 230 British patients.

On the same day as the Irish media were reporting the Dr Elwood case, the British media were reporting on a disciplinary hearing at the General Medical Council against a fifty-two-year-old gynaecologist, Richard Neale. One woman told the inquiry how she suffered pain 'like a cheese wire was cutting inside' in the days following surgery for her incontinence. Another recalled how Dr Neale allegedly reassured her that an operation had been successful, only to change his mind the next day and tell her she might need a kidney removed.

Another case that provoked media controversy was that of a disgraced former gynaecologist, the late Rodney Ledward. The doctor was struck off the medical register in Britain by the General Medical Council. He left Britain to live in Mallow, County Cork, having botched a series of operations on women. At the time of his death, in October 2000, Kent police were investigating dozens of allegations of criminal assault relating to his former patients. Six men had claimed that their wives died after being treated by him and hundreds more are suing for compensation.

The conviction of the Manchester GP, Dr Harold Shipman, who was given fifteen life sentences for the multiple murder of his patients, has no parallel in Ireland in modern times, but there are questions about the monitoring of doctors' performance in this case that transcend geographical boundaries. After sentence was passed it emerged that British police had compiled evidence linking Shipman to the deaths of up to 146 other patients. Shipman began to self-destruct in 1976 when he started to self-medicate with pethidine, an injectable opiate. He began forging prescriptions to feed his habit. There was evidence of peer review as some of his colleagues reported him to the General Medical Council, and he was found guilty of professional misconduct. Public disquiet about the case was accentuated when it emerged that Shipman was not struck off the medical register. The GMC ordered Shipman to undergo treatment but did not rescind his licence to practise. This enabled Shipman to move to a different area and to relaunch his career as a doctor.

They are by no means the first such cases to cause public concern. Many people will recall the well-documented case of the death of the young American woman, Kimberley Bergalis, who died in December 1991, having contracted AIDS in 1987 from her dentist during treatment. It is not my place to adjudicate on such cases, but the series of allegations highlight the need for effective monitoring of the medical profession.

The Experience Down Under

Doctors have professional autonomy. This creates the potential for abuses of power. Rather than trying to pre-empt any ongoing inquires in Ireland to illustrate the dangers of the profession monitoring the actions of its members sufficiently, I will consider a case study of a judicial inquiry into inadequate treatment of cervical cancer in Auckland, New Zealand in 1988. In the Irish context this Report is of interest since it carries implications that extend way beyond New Zealand and the treatment of cervical cancer, as it raises the larger questions of the power of the medical profession and the control of that power.

The constraints of space preclude me from giving a detailed account of the allegations of failures of treatment at the National Women's Hospital, Auckland. However, in a thumbnail sketch the details are as follows. In April 1987 it was alleged in the media that over a period of up to twenty years women with a particular form of cervical cancer, known as cancer in situ (CIS), had, without their knowledge or consent, unwittingly taken part in a research study intended to prove that their condition would not advance to more serious forms of invasive cancer and that, as a consequence, they had failed to get the treatment they needed to prevent the spread of cancer. The Inquiry painstakingly trawled its way through a massive volume of written and oral evidence in an attempt to identify how the deficiencies in treatment occurred and why they continued, apparently unchecked, for such a lengthy period. It was clear that the deep conviction of one consultant regarding the lack of invasive potential of CIS, although queried by several colleagues, was allowed to prevail. This doctor resolutely believed that what he was doing was in the best interests of the patients, that more extensive treatment was superfluous and that his medical assessments about the non-progression of the condition were empirically grounded. It emerged that the convention that medical colleagues were allowed 'clinical freedom' took precedence over all other pressures to intervene.

It was clearly revealed that not only did the consultant in charge exercise huge power over his junior staff and the other professionals in his team, but also that his position was constantly shielded by the senior members of the medical establishment, buttressing him from critics over the years and making it virtually impossible for any non-medical person even to start to yield some influence on the decision-making process. In such circumstances professional autonomy was no more than a euphemism for the abuse of power.

The abuse was compounded by the doctor's failure to nurture the autonomy of his patients. By describing his research study as 'treatment' instead of experimentation and by persistently assuring his patients that they had no reason for concern, the practitioner failed to give the women involved the chance to evaluate the risks and benefits for themselves and thereby to give an educated consent to their participation. Even if the eventual outcome had proved to be entirely beneficial for the patients, in ethical terms the end did not justify the means for this reason. An ethical research study must both protect and enhance the autonomy of the patients who are the subjects of the study.

Despite representations to the medical authorities and despite the report of a special working party, which indicated some cause for concern in at least some cases, the treatment policy of patients under his care was permitted to remain largely unchanged until he retired. Clinical freedom held pre-eminence: peer review, when it was tentatively attempted, was toothless.

The investigating judge pulled no punches:

> I have been drawn inexorably to the conclusion that although there was increasing opposition to the . . . trial, both internationally and at National Women's Hospital, there was no will to confront and resolve the difficult issues that emerged.

> For twenty years there was criticism, yet no special effort was made to ensure that patients' health did not suffer. . . . The medical profession failed in its basic duty to its patients.

The judge went on to advocate a more rigorous system of 'peer review':

> Peer review is possible, given the right spirit and environment and the encouragement and support of administrators. But it should be established in a formal setting. The profession can no longer rely on informal discussions, which may or may not include all relevant members. . . . An inquiry into medical practice is one form of peer review, albeit enforced. It is also the most disastrous for the profession, for patients and for the public purse. I believe that unless the profession can establish adequate peer review and adequate systems to cope with the inevitable mistakes or problems caused by incompetence, then there will be a continuing succession of inquires of this nature.[1]

At the end of her Report the judge offered her thoughts on how such situations should be prevented in the future. She advocated a radical revision of the control of clinical practice and clinical research and the appointment of a 'patient advocate' in research or teaching and to ensure adequate communication with patients.

The Auckland experience suggests that the medical profession are less interested in enhancing the autonomy of those they serve as they are in protecting their own freedom of action. Patients were used as an aim instead of seen as an end, and kept powerless by forces they could not change because they were excluded from the decision-making process. It also calls into question the idea of clinical freedom. As J.R. Hampton, Professor of Cardiology in Nottingham, insightfully observed:

> Clinical freedom is dead, and no one need regret its passing. Clinical freedom was the right – some seemed to believe the divine right – of doctors to do whatever in their opinion was best for their patients. In the days when investigation was non-

existent and treatment as harmless as it was ineffective, the doctor's opinion was all that there was, but now opinion is not good enough.[2]

It is a cliché that power corrupts and that absolute power corrupts absolutely. Powerlessness is as absolute as power. It does not corrupt but it is as destructive, because it dehumanises.

The Professionals

No two doctors will agree on every aspect of care for every patient in every circumstance. Hence the oft quoted maxim, 'Doctors differ and patients die'. It is not always easy to decide what constitutes unprofessional conduct. What should a patient who has received harmful treatment be told? In deciding on whether a particular course of action represents good professional conduct or otherwise, should the professional's action be determined by the standards of the community or by the fear of litigation, by the 'golden rule' or by personal convictions?

The ethical basis of the doctor-patient relationship through the centuries has been outlined in the Hippocratic Oath and its sequels in the form of the Geneva, Helsinki and Tokyo Declarations. The medical profession also has its own professional code set out by the relevant statutory or voluntary regulators of those professions.

In Ireland under the terms of the Medical Practitioners Act 1978 the medical profession is regulated by the Medical Council of Ireland. It consists of twenty-five members, comprising five appointed by the authorities of the undergraduate medical schools, six representing medical and surgical specialities, psychiatry and general practice, ten registered medical practitioners elected by the profession, and four other persons appointed by the Minister for Health, including at least three lay members to represent the interests of the general public. The members hold office for five years. The Medical Council has a myriad of functions, including: the registration of medical practitioners; the maintenance of a register of medical practitioners; control of standards of education and training at undergraduate and post-graduate levels; determination of questions of professional misconduct or fitness to practise, and the operation of EU directives pertaining to education and training in the practice of medicine.

In addition the Council is obliged to give guidance to the medical profession generally on all matters relating to ethical conduct and behaviour. It has issued *A Guide to Ethical Conduct and Behaviour* for registered medical practitioners. While it does not provide a catalogue of either acceptable or unacceptable behaviour, it offers general principles of ethical conduct. It emphasises the 'long and honourable tradition of service and care within the medical profession, and the responsibility of each doctor to uphold this tradition and to maintain high standards'.

A survey of many codes of the medical profession suggests that the health-care professions in general are prone to expressing broad ethical principles, which are normally articulated in the form of imperatives, and that most of these imperatives are vague and of limited value, since they do not go beyond the fundamental humanitarian concerns we would expect of every member of society. A brief survey of the literature of the medical associations highlights the fact that a philanthropic approach to ethics is operative in the medical profession, in that the profession makes an apparently gratuitous pledge to serve the good of the patient. Few would deny the value of philanthropy; however, the medical profession offers no justification for a philanthropic approach to the practice of medicine nor any criteria as to how this philanthropy is to be applied in the profession.

An essential weakness of the philanthropic approach is the failure to acknowledge the indebtedness of the profession to society. The symbiotic relationship of giving and receiving, which is at work in the professional relationship, needs acknowledgement to avoid what in fact occurs in most ethical codes in the medical profession: the expression of a gratuitous service to humanity and an orientation to self-protection. Arguably this approach succumbs to the conceit of philanthropy when it is assumed that the professional commitment to others is purely gratuitous, rather than a responsive or reciprocal act. Without acknowledgement of the professional's prior indebtedness to the community, statements about service to humankind run the risk of being tainted with the odour of condescension, particularly if these documents fail to acknowledge the profession's indebtedness to the socio-political community for gifts such as self-regulation. This raises questions about the adequacy of the ethical philosophy underlying the codes of the various medical associations.

Moral obligation should be considered as a socially constructed practice, as something we learn through the actual experience of trying to live with other people. We are not social because we are moral; we are moral because we live together with others and therefore need periodically to account for who we are. Both professionals and patients are part of a wider social fabric, which must inevitably consider medicine as a profession and society as a political structure. Modern medicine is in fact the creation of society because public investment in the education of health-care professionals and medicine is now a *de facto* part of society's explicit political response to the general predicament of the human person. Society has begun to invest in and use medicine for the general political purposes of the community. Medicine has become a social or civil instrument, and in that sense medicine is now socialised. Medicine has been employed to affect the conditions of society, e.g. change infant mortality rates, enable a population explosion, provide contraception, make life in cities possible without frequent fatal epidemics, etc., and it has thereby become an instrument of society in the sense of publicly supported means of affecting publicly chosen goals. The compass of modern medicine is a political creation. As a result, physicians accrue both rights and duties. They acquire duties to society regarding particular patients. This social nature of medicine serves to transform the traditional context of the doctor–patient relationship, bringing additional far-reaching obligations to the health-care profession. In the contemporary world the profession(al) is greatly indebted to society (e.g. for education and privileges) and to patients past and present, e.g. for research. While society promises that it will grant a virtual monopoly to the profession, with the consequent opportunity for significant personal gain, the profession and its members have consequent responsibilities to society.

In the Dock

We ascribe a special competence in health matters to doctors. Yet it is the profession alone that judges when such competence has been achieved. How do we justify granting such a degree of freedom of decision to an occupational group? The public can only surmise whether the profession is providing what it claims to provide, either by observing what appears to be successes in health care or being content that the number of mistakes is minimal. Such judgements are based on supposition rather than on documentary evidence. The problem is magnified by the propensity of professions to conceal the errors of their incompetent members. In fairness, the Irish Medical Council, to its credit, has produced good discussion documents in the area of competence and has suggested that doctors may require regular fitness-to-practice tests once they reach a certain age. The Irish College of General Practitioners too has been to the forefront in this area. The medical profession seems ready to embrace the concept of revalidation. The time, though, has surely come to move beyond talk and to put a reaccreditation process in place as soon as possible.

Public debate needs specific information about the real situation in medical practice. Transparency, like beauty, often is in the eye of the beholder. The Irish Medical Council would claim to be fully transparent. Medical journalists would not be so sure and would cite the Council's unwillingness to supply the agenda of its AGM to the media as one indication of its lack of transparency. In fairness to the Medical Council, it would be inappropriate for the press to receive the full agenda, which names all the doctors who have become the subject of investigations on foot of complaints. Some of these names include doctors whose reputations have been unjustly tarnished by people making spurious or false claims of incompetence.

The international experience to date is that it is not the medical profession that supplies a clear indication of the reality of medical practice but the media or the publication of important books. In 1985 when the French oncologist Léon Schwartzenberg published *Requiem pour la vie* about his philosophical and personal reflections on his experiences assisting terminally ill patients to die, his book became an immediate bestseller in France and precipitated a major national debate about euthanasia. A similar debate developed in the United States in the same year following the publication of Betty Rollin's *Last Wish,* in which she wrote about helping her terminally ill mother take a fatal overdose. Six years later Derek Humphry's bestselling self-help book, *Final Exit: The Practicalities of Self-deliverance and Assisted Suicide for the Dying,* published by the Hemloch Society, took the debate still further. In Ireland we rely heavily on anecdotal evidence to establish exactly what is going on in medical practice in the country.

Historically, professional ethics has had two main concerns – one concerned with behaviour towards clients, the other with conduct towards colleagues. However, there has always been a tension between obligations to colleagues and to clients. The tendency in the profession has been to take the former duties more seriously than the latter. When concern for peers rather than clients or patients predominates, professional ethics is little more than courtesy within a guild. The profession is obliged to outline the structures by which obligations to colleagues and obligations to clients may be reconciled; for example, the duty of the professional to participate fully in the appropriate professional body and its decision-making and the profession's privilege of self-government.

Professional solidarity has been a major feature of the medical profession in the Western world. While such solidarity is not in itself a problematic issue, an ethical problem arises when professional solidarity interferes with the good of the patient. The historical evidence indicates that the health professions have been too protective of the guild at the expense of the public and, accordingly, can expect to have less decision-making responsibility in evaluating and sanctioning the behaviour of the members.

Moreover, there is evidence to suggest that some professionals allow their profession to do their ethical reflection for them. In an article in the *Guardian* in 1991, for example, Anthony Scrivener was quoted as saying, 'The rules fix my morality for me', and 'It's easy for the lawyer: there are rules. There are lighthouses all along the route for me and I haven't got to make moral judgements as I go.'

What these comments indicate is the belief that the legal profession has rules that leave no room for ethical decision-making of the individual and that moral claims do not arise with regard to these rules. This is a view that cannot remain uncontested. However, it is imperative for it to be reflected upon within the profession rather than simply from outside.

The medical profession in Ireland needs far more accountability and transparency than we have got to date. There are obstacles to the achievement of this at the moment, e.g. the Ombudsman does not have the power to investigate cases involving public voluntary hospitals. As things stand, we are relying almost completely on the profession to police itself.

Private Eyes

Peer review is designed to monitor the technical performance and skills of colleagues who may not be performing up to acceptable standards, thereby helping to ensure that the best interests of the patient and the profession are safeguarded. However, as we have seen, it is the profession itself that determines what is reasonably regarded as professional or unprofessional conduct in any given case and, more fundamentally, what are the rules, written or unwritten, governing the profession. This raises a number of potential problems. Are professional codes always grounded on ethical principles? Does professional duty become no more than what the profession says it is? Matters affecting society cannot be left solely to the interests of professionals because patients and society need to be safeguarded also. The manner in which doctors responsible, or suspected of being responsible, for unprofessional conduct are threatened by their fellow professionals is also an area that merits ethical reflection in its own right. There have to be provisions that will ensure that peer review is not used as a pretext for unfairly excluding or limiting the practice of professional colleagues. Where possible, discipline should be applied 'gently' so that individuals might be encouraged and strengthened and so that every possible opportunity for amendment might be given where necessary. Criticism by professionals of other professionals, or disciplinary action, should always be tempered with compassion, particularly in the case of doctors who have fallen prey to substance abuse or psychiatric problems, for example. Much more problematic are the cases of doctors who may lack the requisite knowledge or technical ability and refuse to seek remedy for their deficiencies. At the moment, the system does not adequately discriminate between the two categories.

Doctors are ethically obliged to report 'incompetence' of other professionals, as the profession correctly articulates the view that patient safety is the doctor's overriding concern; however, the doctor is also faced with the obligation to maintain the image of profession. In the vast majority of cases both goals sit very comfortably with each other, but when a patient suffers because of a doctor's 'incompetence' they may be mutually exclusive. Perhaps the most fundamental weakness in the codes of the medical profession in this area is that it fails to offer any guidance as to how the doctor might reconcile such incompatible goals.

A crucial concern from the public's point of view is the efficacy of peer review in promoting ethically responsible behaviour in medicine. One statistic that highlights the scale of the problem is that there were only six dentists expelled from the American Dental Association over a two-year period (1981 and 1982), despite the fact that in the Unites States there were 117,223 dentists practising. Moreover, these sanctions were in relation to membership of the Association and it cannot be determined from official sources whether loss of licensure to practise ensued. This illustration raises the question: just how seriously does the medical profession take their responsibilities in the area of peer review to report instances of gross and continual faulty treatment by other practitioners? Is there a laxity in self-government that forces the question of its validity and effectiveness?

So what are doctors to do when they discover that a colleague's work is incompetent or unethical? Self-interest may dictate that the intelligent option is to do nothing – otherwise the doctor's livelihood or career prospects or standing in the profession is jeopardised. Hamlet's dilemma was 'to be or not to be'. Increasingly, health-care professionals may find that their dilemma is 'to speak or not to speak'.

Whistleblowing

The individual's obligation to avoid complicity in harmful, corrupt or fraudulent activities is considered an important part of professional responsibility. Should the doctor who notices that a colleague has been negligent therefore engage in 'whistleblowing'? Whistleblowing is the act of an individual sounding an alarm within her or his working environment, in order to expose neglect or abuses that jeopardise public interest.

For many people the idea of informing seems invidious. However, should a doctor's freedom to practise take precedence over patient safety, once a threat to that safety has been clearly established?

Whistleblowing presents a major dilemma for this doctor, because to act on the duty of nonmaleficence to the community and inform on colleagues' negligence conflicts with the person's loyalty to these colleagues whose professional reputations, career and livelihood would be threatened by such an action. The consequences to their families would also have to be considered.

The tension between openness and secrecy is an integral part of everyday life. As Sissela Bok incisively observes in perhaps the definitive work in this area:

> Any inquiry into the ethics of secrecy must consider the conflicts that we all experience in making such choices: between keeping secrets and revealing them; between wanting to penetrate the secrets of others and to leave them undisturbed; and between responding to what they reveal to us and ignoring or even denying it. These conflicts are rooted in the most basic experience of what it means to live as one human being among others, needing both to hide and to share, both to seek out and to beware of the unknown.[3]

Professional solidarity becomes unethical when it interferes with the safety of the public. Silence is not always golden. The International Committee of the Red Cross kept silent about Hitler's plans to exterminate the Jews, when it had relevant and reliable information about his many excesses. Part of the official Red Cross defence after the war was that the organisation was irrevocably committed to confidentiality and neutrality. Of course the ethical issues involved in that case were complex, but does their defence stand up to the full rigours of ethical scrutiny? In medicine as in any walk of life, keeping aloof ultimately involves complicity. It is equally important in our era of 'accountability and transparency' that questions of peer review are discussed publicly, otherwise unnecessary anxiety will be generated.

Perhaps one small step forward would be the involvement of patients in ethics committees in hospitals. Patient involvement in ethics committees offers advantages both to the patient and the profession. Patients would have a forum to voice their own ethical insights and would develop a greater technical knowledge of medicine and gain a greater appreciation of the practical problems of doctors. Doctors would benefit from receiving a broader level of ethical insights and also from a better doctor-patient relationship, as patients would be better informed and consequently more sympathetic to the practical problems of the doctor in day-to-day practice.

Notes

1.   New Zealand Government Printing Office, *The Report of the Cervical Cancer Inquiry,* Committee of Inquiry into Allegations Concerning the Treatment of Cervical Cancer at National Women's Hospital and into Other Related Matters, Auckland, New Zealand, 1988.

2.   J.R. Hampton, 'The End of Clinical Freedom', *British Medical Journal,* Vol. 287 (1983), p. 1237.

3.   Sissela Bok, *Secrets: On the Ethics of Concealment and Revelation* (New York, Random House, 1983), p. xvi.

6

THE DOCTOR'S DILEMMA

When Imelda Marcos was first lady of the Philippines she had a dream. She wanted to turn her country into the world capital for heart transplant operations – a perfectly admirable aspiration. The problem was that to achieve her ambition she proposed to divert practically all her country's health budget to finance these state-of-the-art facilities. As a result the budget for primary health care for the entire population would have been on a par with her personal budget for shoes. Her grandiose plans had to be shelved on foot of the tidal wave of outrage her proposal generated. It was almost universally accepted that treatment for the privileged few should not be at the expense of the impoverished many.

A study of ethical issues in the health-care professions presents a number of problems. New ethical issues are constantly emerging because of technical advances in health care and societal changes that have brought new ethical dilemmas. The accent and main emphasis of the health-care professions in general has changed from being predominantly an evaluation of the encounter between the professional and the patient to a consideration of wider issues. These issues extend much further than what happens in the 'doctor's chair' to a reflection on the broader context in which medicine finds itself.

In a sense medical ethics is principally concerned with what health-care professionals ought to do when they are not sure what to do. Some of the ethical questions that arise because of this wider context include: Which patients should have priority when a particular health resource is scarce? There are not only questions concerning certain medical procedures, but also difficult questions of priorities in the allocation of available funds, e.g. between preventive medicine and treatment of illness. How is the tension between the rights of individual patients and the overall good of society to be resolved?

What are the relevant inequalities that justify giving more of the scarce resources to some potential patients and less to others? At its starkest, two questions present themselves: Who shall be treated when not all can be treated? Who shall live when not all can live?

In Alexander Solzhenitsyn's novel *Cancer Ward,* there is an interesting exchange when Shulubin is talking to Kostoglotov:

> Kostoglotov then raises questions. 'There has to be an economy after all, doesn't there? That comes before anything else.' 'Does it?' said Shulubin. 'That depends. For example, Vladimir Solovyov argues rather convincingly that an economy could and should be built on an ethical basis.'
>
> 'What's this? Ethics first and economics afterwards?' Kostoglotov looked bewildered.

There is an ongoing tension in the health-care system between what is the 'right thing' economically and the right thing ethically. In the Irish context, one person's experience may serve to illustrate.

Annie's Song
Annie Ryan is a former president of the National Association for Mentally Handicapped of Ireland and has been a tireless campaigner for the rights of people with disabilities. She is author of *Walls of Silence,* an account of attitudes to people with a mental disability and of the dealings of successive governments in this area.

> I first became interested in disability issues when our eldest son, Tom, wasn't progressing as we knew he should. He was born in 1964 and could walk and looked perfect but he couldn't talk. It was quite clear when he was four years of age that he had something drastically wrong with him. We brought him to the child guidance unit in the Mater and he was diagnosed as having autistic phenomena. They tried to get us access to some kind of service because they recognised that Tom was going to be very difficult for us to manage on our own but I remember them saying very forcibly, 'Don't mention he's autistic whatever you do.'

We lived in Sligo at the time and there was a big mental handicap centre just outside the town. We applied for Tom to get a place there. They said no but eventually they agreed to take him on trial for a month in the mornings. At the end of the month we were told, 'No way.' I'll never forget the sense of rejection. I felt my son was rejected and that I was rejected. I happened to know the bishop at the time, Bishop Hanly, who was a lovely man, and I told him what had happened and he said, 'I can't believe it. That's why I brought them here. Will I make them do it?' One of the teachers said, 'No you can't do it because all they will do is ignore him.'

After that we tried to manage at home but Tom was disturbed all day and all night. We reached a stage where we couldn't cope on our own anymore and we were told there never would be the facilities we needed in Sligo. So we moved to Dublin. We got Tom into a school all right but only for a year. When the year was up we were told he would not be taken back.

We went to a psychiatrist and he said there were no facilities for him in Dublin and then he said, 'If he were my son I'd send him to the Rudolph Steiner school in Belfast.' I remember the day we brought Tom up for the first time I knew there was something strange going on. It was the day before internment was introduced.

When he was younger Tom kept our family very busy but not so busy that we did not notice that there were huge inequalities and anomalies in the way certain people with mental disability were treated. Where our family lives and have done since we had to move in search of a school which would accept our son, there was a large residential school for slow learners. These could, with a little organisation, have been catered for in a day school in their own community. For five years we passed that school at least twelve times a year on our way to and from Belfast where we found a school which would accept our son. He was not the only child who had to travel to Belfast to avail of his constitutional right. Why?

After five years Tom couldn't be kept in Belfast because he developed epilepsy and they hadn't appropriate facilities to deal with that there. There was no place, so at the age of twelve, we sent him as a last resort to St Ita's, Portrane.

We decided though that we were not going just to leave him there. We were going to find out exactly what was wrong with the system that people like Tom had to end up in Portrane. We met with parents and we discovered that there was a large number of people around the country with a mental handicap who had nowhere to go except a mental hospital. We started to get to know what the conditions were like in Portrane and they were horrifying.

When Tom went to St Ita's Hospital in 1976 we stumbled on a scandal which had been going on for a long time. The conditions in many of the mental hospitals were appalling and were known to quite a few. Yet one never heard a word about them. Why?

The State invested heavily in the general hospitals during the 1950s and the 1960s, at the same time grant aiding the voluntary system. All this laudable activity was in stark contrast to the treatment which was thought affordable for the long-stay patients in the mental hospitals.

In the late 1950s towns were proud of their hospitals. Every Sunday they were thronged by the visiting relatives of the patients and every day there was constant coming and going. During those same years the mental hospitals stood lonely and unvisited, their isolation reflecting the rejection of their inmates by families and friends. It was a rejection that went deep into our society – as high as the President of the High Court.

St Ita's Hospital had started out its long life as 'Portrane Lunatic Asylum', built in the last years of the last century to relieve overcrowding at the other much older lunatic asylum at Grangegorman. The new Asylum was a vast undertaking. It was planned to accommodate some 1200 patients. Sited on the sea coast and commanding magnificent views, it was a most impressive edifice. In the years since it had been built it changed little except its name. In 1925 it became known as Portrane Mental Hospital. In 1958 it shared in the general sanctification of the fifties and was re-named St Ita's.

Close to the hospital were the wooden huts which had been used by the workmen who had built the hospital. In 1903 it had been decided by the joint committee which ran the hospital that they would retain those wooden buildings in case they were ever needed again. By 1904 one of the wooden buildings had been put into use again. All six were in use by 1966. There were 200 or so people with a mental handicap in those huts. Tom was twelve so he was in a children's ward which meant he was okay.

One of the problems was that it was very difficult to find out about St Ita's at the time. One of the people who wanted to find out was Dr John O'Connell TD. As a TD and as a medical doctor he had a special interest in this area but when he went out to visit St Ita's he was frogmarched out by two nurses without getting the opportunity to find anything.

A programme of refurbishment was completed in the early 1980s and the patients were finally moved out of the notorious huts in 1982. The newly refurbished units were an enormous improvement on the old festering eye-sores, but the old mental hospital lay-outs survived. Mentally disabled people were still condemned to hour after hour in the large day rooms. They slept at night in the long dormitories. The numbers were still high.

In February 1982 at the height of a snow blizzard the hospital was without electricity for a period of thirty-one hours. The generator at the hospital was inadequate and so there was no heat or light at the hospital. I understand that the nurses put all the patients to bed, sedated them and watched over them in their overcoats using torches for light. Not a word of this ever reached the papers, although up to a thousand patients were involved. The papers were full of news of the blizzard and were particularly concerned about the plight of the sheep in the Wicklow hills. I was at home in the suburbs and I was told what was going on. I tried to ring Michael O'Leary who was Tánaiste at the time because the Taoiseach, Garret Fitzgerald, was out of the country. At the time he was called the Minister for Snow but I couldn't get through to him. I rang up one of my neighbours who was an army officer and explained the situation to him. He said that's the kind of thing the army is for so the following day the faulty generator was replaced by the army.

It was in this manner that almost any progress in Portrane was achieved. After each crisis, usually involving some exposure in the media, the particular aspect of abuse would be addressed. This was a slow way to improve a service. It was particularly slow in Portrane as the policy of emptying the hospitals, including St Ita's, Portrane, gathered momentum. No effort was made to break up the over-large units. The minimum was spent on hospital maintenance. There was no attempt made to extend therapies to cover a large number of mentally disabled. Large numbers of people with a mental disability never left the dreary rooms except to go to bed, especially if the weather was bad. As the Eastern Health Board put it in their report on the services at St Ita's Hospital:

> Since 1980 we have had an ongoing policy of transferring the less dependent residents from St Ita's. However, the vacated places were immediately filled by highly dependent patients, mainly disturbed.

In spite of the scandal of the huts and in spite of all the hopes of establishing a service at St Ita's, Portrane, the hospital had retained its function as a dumping ground for the rejected people from the other services. As the Eastern Health Board put it:

> This has been largely to do with the fact that the emphasis has been on devoting the limited resources available to the needs of the less disturbed mentally handicapped. . . . Most mentally handicapped persons with seriously disturbed behaviour invariably end up being admitted to St Ita's and become long stay residents.

I found no villains anywhere. On the contrary one could not be but impressed by the hard work and dedication of those in charge of the services. How could so many honourable people who were undoubtedly charitable and competent, allow such a situation to develop?

One answer might be that our political system, even our constitution, does not adequately protect the helpless, certainly if they are less than visible. And that prompts the most likely explanation of all. The reticence with which the issue of mental disability has been approached does not help. When people have no voice, silence is not always golden.

Many thousands have died in the mental hospitals since the authorities ceased to pay any attention to reports on their conditions. It is right that we should remember them. For those people who died, well within living memory, the only fitting memorial would be the determination that such a state of affairs should never happen again.

Tom is thirty-six now. The awful thing is that there are people who are going through now what we went through with Tom thirty years ago. I met a woman three weeks ago whose nineteen-year-old daughter was sent back to them and there is nowhere left for her but St Ita's, Portrane. All around Ireland there are parents with disabled children who are asking the question: what will happen to my child when I die?

What will our children be ashamed about when they look back in forty years at the state of Irish society in the early years of the third millennium? In the light of Annie Ryan's testimony the intolerable condition of many people with severe disabilities in Ireland should be obvious to all. For all our talk of equal rights, a significant minority of such people living in Ireland have not significantly improved their lot or achieved legal, economic or cultural parity. The economic, political and cultural disadvantages suffered by these Celtic Tiger outcasts are serious violations of justice.

One of the big buzz phrases today in social and political life is the democratic deficit – the frustration 'ordinary people' have because they are denied any real power in the society they live in, with little or no say in the decision-making processes. For the disabled person the possibility of making decisions for themselves is often little more than a pipe dream. Decisions about their welfare are often taken by people who have no direct experience of what it is like to be disabled.

Much lip-service is paid to the disabled, which fails to yield any practical benefits. The problem is resources, or more precisely lack of resources. Many medical and technical advances have presented new and exciting treatment options – the use of art and music therapy to help people cope with mental illness is just one such innovative example. However, there is a major shortage of funding, which leaves many disabled people seriously disadvantaged. It is too easy, though, to talk about action for disabled people in terms of aspirations. What is needed are specific targets and specific action programmes.

Swift Medicine

As if to confirm the contemporary relevance of Annie Ryan's assessment, on 2 August 2000 the Inspector of Mental Hospitals, Dr Dermot Walsh, issued his Report for 1999. He referred to the 'generally unsatisfactory standard' of St Ita's and drew attention to the fact that the hospital was 'under stress' because it provides for several hundred learning-disability patients.

While the picture that emerged was one of slow progress the report pulled in no punches in its comments on a number of other hospitals. In a hospital in Leinster the Report observed, 'The whole situation in the admissions unit was intolerable and could not be condoned.' Almost a third of the patients in the hospital had 'an intellectual disability and required specialist care in an intellectual disability facility' and 'were inappropriately placed'. Parents were 'not satisfied with aspects of privacy and dignity of care in the admissions unit'.

Historically, the mentally ill and disabled have been seen by the law as unworthy of equal treatment. Until the eighteenth century the mentally disabled were not treated as such but instead shut away from society's intolerant eye in workhouses or prisons. In the Irish context it was not until 1757 with the opening of St Patrick's Hospital in Dublin that provision was made for the care of the mentally disabled

through a provision in the will of Jonathan Swift. He described his
bequest as:

> He gave the little Wealth he had,
> to build a House for Fools and mad:
> And show'd by one satyric Touch,
> No nation wanted it so much.

T. S. Szasz, in *The Myth of Mental Illness: Foundations of a Theory of
Personal Conduct* (1974), argues that 'mental illness' is nothing but a
label used to control those who do not conform to society's ideal of
accepted behaviour. In this perspective, psychiatry is a form of social
control.

There are many thorny legal and ethical problems in the area of
mental illness: notably in the involuntary incarceration of patients and
the validity of consent to particular forms of treatment. The problems
are exacerbated by the fact that much of the legislation in this area is
very old, e.g. the Trial of Lunatics Act 1883. In this area, like many
others, we must strive for legislation that maximises the fulfilment of
rights and minimises their violations. Incredibly, though, in the
Ireland of the Celtic Tiger there are many people with disabilities
whose lives could be transformed with basic treatment – but there is
insufficient money.

It's More than Words

The ability to talk easily and communicate in this day and age is one
of the most important social skills. On the face of it somebody with a
difficulty in this area would appear to have little possibility of rising to
the top of the political tree. Yet Proinsias de Rossa has done just that
despite the apparent handicap of a stammer. His speech problems
manifested themselves at an early age.

> I remember that I first became aware of the problem when I
> moved from the infant's to 'the Master's' as we used call it.
> Possibly because of changes in the teaching methods my mother
> came down to the school when I moved to first class to explain

that I had this problem and that he should take care to deal with me in a sensitive way. I have to say that for a while I took advantage of it! I became very conscious of it around seven years of age. For a long time afterwards I'd have great difficulty using phones and even getting a job.

Like many people in my situation I had to cope with an intense and particular form of shyness. I'm not sure was the shyness the cause of the stammer or the stammer the cause of the shyness but certainly I was very aware of it. It was fine when I was in the bosom of my family but I was much more aware of it when I was out in the streets playing with my friends and they obviously made comments about it. As they got to know me better they stopped talking about it but other people who were new to me often commented on it and naturally this made me very self-conscious especially as I got older and started getting interested in girls.

I was especially fortunate in that my family had particular insights into speech impediments. I was the only one of the children in our family to have a stammer but almost uniquely my mother had one as well. I grew up therefore in a very supportive environment. I tended to spend a lot of time in the local library. A stammer can have a profound effect on how you make friends. A lot of people can have no problems speaking when they are in the company of their friends but when they meet new people it can be very awkward particularly when there is ignorance of what being a stammerer involves.

I was talking to somebody recently for the first time and he told me that when he heard that I was running for election to the Dáil he said to myself, 'Oh my God, that man will never be elected because he has a bad stammer', but I was! I know people who can't get jobs even though they have only mild stammers. Some employers have very narrow attitudes to people who have a stammer.

I have never availed of the services of a speech therapist. When I was young it was something that people didn't think about. Even if there were facilities available we had twelve in the family and when I was born in 1940 we didn't have the money to pay for it.

It's not a new problem. I'm told that Moses had a stammer. I use the joke that if he hadn't a stammer we'd only have two commandments because he was forced to use a lot of word substitution!

I am patron of the Irish Stammering Association (their phone number is 01-2847040) and am quite keen not only to help people understand the problem but to urge that more resources be provided particularly for children to cope with the problem. There are many people who are literally living lives of quiet desperation because of a stammer. I've got many, many letters to prove that. One of the saddest parts of my life is when I get heart-rending letters from people who have stammers and who because of that are unable to make social connections. Some people in this situation can have very few friends. I know there are people out there whose lives have been shattered because they didn't get the help they needed.

Our economy is awash with money and the amount of money that would be required to help people out in this situation is relatively minor. It's not that it is going to be a growing expenditure in the years ahead. I don't like overloading the schools but I think the prejudice that people with speech difficulties experience is an issue that should be addressed there. I would also like to see GPs more sensitive to people in this category. Although it is not a disease or a physical disability people think it's not important but it can have a huge effect on people's self-development.

ER

Having considered the problem of equity in the health service from the outside it is instructive to consider the problem from a doctor's perspective. Dr Leonard Condren is a GP and a former medical editor of *Forum*.

I'm working in Ballyfermot where there are a lot of patients on medical cards although I would have a significant number who are private patients. Purely by chance two women in their early sixties came into me with advanced arthritis problems. One person was on the medical card; one was in the VHI. The person in the VHI got a letter of referral and was seen by a specialist within six to eight weeks and once seen was admitted to a private hospital. Her hip would have been replaced within three months of seeing me.

The other lady was on a medical card and she would have to go through the public outpatients system. She would probably be waiting at least a year before she gets to see a specialist and then she waits a year before she gets surgery. It never ceases to amaze me why the point isn't made more loudly that there are actually two waiting lists: the waiting list before you get to the specialist and the waiting list before you get surgery. She has to wait two years or more. In that time she will be attending me and I will be prescribing various combination of tablets to see if they can alleviate the problem. Just as an aside I saw an amusing thing on television recently from one of the Art Colleges in Britain where a student made a collage of pills which was the amount of pills that a person would take from the first time they are seen to the time they have their operation.

What people don't realise is that the waiting list is very inefficient because it's a huge waste of resources. While she will have her knee replaced eventually, she's coming down to me regularly and saying that her pills aren't working. The State has paid for all this medication and it's an enormous waste of my time. I've made the diagnosis two years earlier but I'm sustaining her through increasing pain and disability. They are taking somebody else's place in surgery and it's enormously wasteful to provide sub-optimum treatment for people who are simply marking time as they wait for the surgery they need.

You come across these inequalities all the time. To take the example of varicose veins I've lost track of how long it takes now. We got a circular every so often from hospitals to enquire if the person is still in need of surgery – where they are reviewing their waiting lists – and inevitably they are.

The nurses' strike and junior doctors' strike are symptomatic of something that is wrong in the medical profession – quite apart from their grievances over pay and conditions. There are junior hospital doctors leaving in steady numbers. There will be places in the not too distant future where there will not be doctors to serve and inevitably they will be in the areas with the greatest socio-economic deprivation. Social inequality creates ill-health in the first place. Doctors will be clustered around the lucrative watering-holes rather than dispersed through the blackspots, as has happened in most developed countries.

Dr Condren's example presents a microcosm of a much broader issue: the allocation of scarce resources. An example, loosely based on a real situation, may serve to illustrate the issues at stake. Dr Fiona Lennon has just been appointed the head of a new dialysis unit in a leading city hospital. She discovers that 893 patients require treatment in the unit. However, the unit is only equipped to treat 650. Dr Lennon is not used to such decisions and seeks the advice of her colleagues. Dr A suggests ability to pay should be the determining issue. Dr B suggests a 'first come first served' policy. Dr C suggests choices be made by a lottery. Dr D suggests that patients should be treated on the basis of their ability to make a positive contribution to society in the future. Dr E suggests that patients should be treated on the basis of their contribution to society in the past. How should she decide?

All Patients Are Equal But Some Are More Equal Than Others

Although most civilised societies espouse the concept of the equality of all, this ideal rarely corresponds with the reality. Issues in the allocation of resources for and within health care are arguably the most difficult areas in a consideration of ethics and medicine today. In health care, situations present themselves in which decisions must be taken and alternatives must be selected that will bring advantage to some and that may leave others disadvantaged. A political ideal, or a constitutional right, might assert that every patient has an equal claim to health, but this aspiration might not be realised; choices need to be made about which patients and which treatments will be given priority. In a situation where there seems to be a contradiction in choosing some, in order that fair advantage may be given to all, then it is essential that we consider, however tentatively, the ethical grounds upon which choices may be made.

There is both an economic and ethical dimension to the problem of allocation. The basic economic problem is how society's scarce resources can be most efficiently allocated, in the light of economic facts and predictions, in order to satisfy human needs and desires. The key ethical dilemma is by what means we can guarantee justice in the distribution of available health resources. Health-care professionals, by virtue of the privileges they receive from patients and society, have corresponding obligations to both. In the context of societal justice and health care, two crucial questions are: how much of society's general wealth will be spent on health care and, secondly, for which purposes will society's money be spent?

A wide variety of approaches to decisions about the distribution of health-care resources present themselves. One suggestion is that an assessment on broad medical suitability should be made by randomisation, either by a lottery or on a first-come first-served system, with appropriate safeguards to ensure that some people could not abuse the system by availing of 'inside knowledge'. The merit of this approach is that everybody has an equal chance. However, this approach reduces complex ethical decisions to random luck.

Another approach is based on the premise: 'to each according to their merit or desert'. Meritorian conceptions are essentially grading ones, advantages are allocated in accordance with amounts of energy expended or kind of results achieved. What is considered is particular conduct that distinguishes persons from one another and not only the fact that all the parties are human beings. A related view begins from the belief that: 'to each according to their societal contribution'.

There are three difficulties common to the meritorian approaches. Firstly, what criteria are to be used to decide non-medical merit? Who decides? Is there a danger of subjective decisions? If so, how can prejudice against groups often discriminated against in particular societies be prevented? A second difficulty with these approaches is a too-ready acceptance of the existing maldistribution of health resources. The imbalance is particularly evident in the privileged access of some to health care because of wealth or position. A third difficulty is the use of pressure. Many groups in society can wield a level of power that is disproportionate to their needs. If decisions about the distribution of scarce resources for health care were to be influenced by political muscle, then groups such as the physically and mentally disadvantaged would do very poorly.

Yet a further approach to decisions about the allocation of scarce resources begins from the premise that the starting point of any such discussion is the need of the individual patient. This is the basis for public health care in Sweden and the National Health Service in Britain. There has been a considerable debate in health-care economics literature on 'need-based' versus 'demand-based' health care. Needs refer to an entire range of interests pertaining to a person's 'psycho-physical existence'. A need is identified with something basic and essential that somebody lacks, both in a physiological and psychological sense. The patient's need is one of support and healing, a need that transcends reward or payment, because the patient is divorced from the world of exchange and enters the world of dependence. This situation is not unique to health care, e.g. in the area of education, there ought not to be a correlation between disposable income and the right of a child to a reasonable education in society.

The two criteria for guidance about such difficult decisions that I wish to defend are medical indication and the belief in the equality of each patient. These two criteria appear to have influenced the World Health Organisation's espousal of medical and dental care for all people in its declaration at the Alma-Ata Conference in 1978:

> Governments have a responsibility for the health of their people which can be fulfilled only by the provision of adequate health and social measures. A main social target of governments, international organizations and the whole world community in the coming decades should be the attainment by all peoples of the world by the year 2000 of a level of health that will permit them to lead a socially and economically productive life.

There are many potential patients in society, all of them having an equal claim to health, because of their innate dignity as human beings. In the Christian perspective all potential patients deserve such equality because of their status as daughters or sons of God. The medical indication shows that the patient has a pressing need for the required treatment, that she or he belongs to that category for which this treatment is specifically intended. It identifies which patient can benefit from which treatment, and if a real promise of improved health exists. The medical claim lies in the condition of the patient and in the realistic hope of what is feasible at any given time, what medical problems can be coped with, what needs can be met. As *The Black Report* in the UK context showed, inequalities in the health service are real. The equality of patients acts as a reminder that having made a judgement about medical priority, then the doctor can only proceed along lines that allow the maximum and most practical availability of health care to each patient. However, these criteria for guidance are not rigid. This is best illustrated by an example. A Bedouin camel owner and a Hollywood movie star may both have a toothache. Clearly both need help and should receive it. This is not to argue that both should receive exactly the same level of dental treatment because the film star would probably be in a position to pay for the most expensive level of treatment available, including 'purely cosmetic' treatment.

It may not be possible to bring full health care to everybody and it may not be possible to tackle every health problem with the same urgency. There may have to be a cut-off point, where the full and just deployment of resources will fall short of some needs. Unfortunately, this does not just apply to health care but to education and employment, indeed to all opportunity. Doctors are challenged by their pledge to play a 'responsible role in the community', to critically examine their own role in the distribution of scarce resources, particularly in the light of past guildlike, monopolistic practices of the health professionals. The medical profession is challenged to ensure that the cut-off point is justly measured, and must be constantly dissatisfied that it leaves some who are out of reach, by its self-imposed claim to serve the good of the patient.

As we noted in a previous chapter, the principle of beneficence imposes an obligation on the health-care professional to benefit the patient. The difficulty is in deciding where the obligation to the patient is to end. Do doctors have an absolute commitment to patient interests that supersedes all other considerations? As tax-payers as well as patients, how many of us would wish to see a situation where doctors could feel free to spend as much as they liked on their patients, regardless of probability of benefit, or scale of the benefit or the cost? Medical ethics in practice recognises a proliferation of potentially conflicting ethical objectives, and seldom are health-care professionals willing or able to sustain a claim that any of those principles must always take precedence over the others, that special obligation to patients does not in practice and should not in theory over-ride all our other ethical obligations, including a general obligation to act justly or fairly.

There Are More Questions Than Answers

Practically all allocation decisions in this area concern the aspects of health to be emphasised and the most effective and efficient means to their realisation. We have to confront the conflict between health care, especially medical care, and some other social goods, not all of which serve as instruments to better health.

Should hospitals always have priority over museums?
This discussion is paralleled to some extent by the argument in health-care economics about whether health care is a 'consumption good' (i.e. we buy it when we are ill just as we buy tea bags when we want to make tea) or an 'investment good' (i.e. good health is like maintaining the value of the house you own. You invest in improvements, building, etc., to give you good housing in the future. Similarly with health care, especially preventive care). This raises another question: what is the role of prevention?

One effort to reconcile ethical and economic considerations has been the debate about ethical dilemmas in relation to the end of life and the development of the principle of QALYs (Quality Adjusted Life Years). In economic utilitarianism QALYs are usually taken as an outcome measure in establishing the cost-effectiveness of the various treatments, i.e. an effort to make the most efficient use of scarce resources by deciding what quality of life a very sick person is likely to have based on a variety of factors such as age, sex, race, past medical history, etc.

Although an exhaustive blueprint for the health care services falls outside the scope of this work, some preliminary observations can be made. In the context of difficult decisions about the distribution of resources in health care, the two criteria that I have suggested as important points of reference are the need for medical care and the equality of patients. However, the very complexity of these issues underlines the importance of a sustained and vigorous debate on the ethical aspects of policies in the distribution of scarce health resources. It may be that medical ethics as we know it is not up to this challenge.

A New Departure
Medicine is practised within a particular historical and cultural milieu and therefore significant societal changes invariably impact on it. The Enlightenment, for example, ushered in a new era of rationalist thought with a consequent diminution of the place and power of religion in human life. The role of medicine and the doctor was defined against this new secular background.

Perhaps the most fundamental change that happened in the organisation of medicine in this period was that the site of medical practice moved from the home to the hospital. For example, in 1873 there were 178 hospitals in the USA; by 1909 there were 4,359 hospitals. This change has profoundly shaped modern medicine. The ground was set for many future clashes between Church and State, and between the medical profession and the emerging non-medical administrators. These flashpoints are still with us.

In addition, hospitals spawned a whole new world of health-care personnel, and there was not always a harmonious relationship between the traditional medical practitioners and the new professionals. In Britain, the social consequences of the industrial revolution saw the emergence of acts like the Sickness Insurance Act of 1883 and the Industrial Accident Act in 1884. This placed the health-care professional in a new and unaccustomed role: no longer merely family friend and confidant(e), the doctor is more bound by the State and caught in the middle ground between the claims of religion, the State and political interests. The thread of unity in the disparate approaches to health care in the nineteenth century is that they appeal to foundations that are open to rational investigation, argument and criticism. They are non-sectarian moral values rather than varieties of religiously oriented, medical ethics.

In the twentieth century there were a number of new ethical issues, such as concern for ethical standards in research and experimentation: while it is right to control and eliminate disease, what are the criteria by which to monitor these? From the 1850s on there was a series of new questions about the beginning of life, abortion and premature babies, and also difficult questions about the seriously ill and dying patient. The high cost of health care raises issues about the distribution of resources. Perhaps the changes can be summed up by saying that the doctor is now less the practitioner of an art than the master (and servant) of a scientific technology. The health-care professional is influenced by the demands of society just as much as by the private relationship with the patient.

These brief examples reflect the growing concern that the development of a social conscience in medicine be complemented by a concern that the ethical issues in medicine be more seriously tackled. The debates on contraception, abortion and euthanasia reflect this trend.

In the United States the changing role of the hospital (birth and death are now more likely to take place here than in the home), the predominance of science and technology (diagnosis and treatment are now largely dictated by laboratory research, which reflects the growth in discoveries about bacteriology, pathology and physiology) and the growing specialisation (in 1964 there were 73,144 GPs, by 1974 this number was down to 53,997) are the main developments. As a result of these far-reaching changes, ethicists became increasingly concerned with the inability of medical ethics, in its traditional form, to situate the ethics of medicine in a wider life context, more adapted to social change and capable of dealing with specialists in an interdisciplinary way. Consequently ethicists began to distinguish between 'medical ethics' and 'bioethics'. Medical ethics is an attempt to decide and make explicit what these duties are or should be for physicians.

Medical ethics is a special kind of ethics only insofar as it relates to a particular realm of facts and concerns and not because it embodies or appeals to some special moral principles and rules that we would appeal to, and argue for, in ordinary circumstances. It is just that in medical ethics these familiar rules are being applied to situations peculiar to the medical world.

Bioethics provides a much wider approach than simply rules of behaviour for a particular guild; it seeks to decide how humankind ought to act in the biomedical realm affecting birth, death, human nature and the quality of life.

Traditionally, ethicists have explored three major normative questions. Firstly, what kinds of action are good? Secondly, what kinds of character are morally praiseworthy? Thirdly, what state of affairs are most worthwhile? Medical ethics attempts to grapple with these questions in the context of the doctor-patient relationship, whereas bioethics can be understood as an effort to raise these questions as they arise in the context of biomedical research and practice. Bioethics itself is a composite term derived from the Greek words *bios* (life) and *ethike* (ethics). One of the first people to use the term was Van R. Potter in his *Bioethics: Bridge to the Future* (1971). Here bioethics has been defined by Potter as the systematic study of human conduct in the area of the life sciences and health care, insofar as this conduct is examined in the light of moral principles and values. It attempts to use the biological and medical sciences to improve the quality of life. It is the 'science for survival' that helps write prescriptions for productive and satisfying lives.

The term 'medical ethics' continues to be used by many influential ethicists and health-care professionals. The term 'medical ethics' offers ethicists three advantages. Firstly, 'medical ethics' attempts to decide and make explicit what are or should be the duties for health-care professionals. Secondly, it makes explicit what could reasonably be expected by patients in their interaction with health-care professionals. Thirdly, it provides society with clear guidelines as to what ethicists and medical personnel consider acceptable or otherwise in the doctor-patient relationship.

Ethical concerns with medicine often stray beyond narrowly defined issues of medicine. Bioethics stretches medicine's remit far beyond its own capacity to cure and seeks to prevent illness and to create the best possible conditions for the health of the whole human community. Bioethics encompasses medical ethics but extends beyond the customary ethical problems of the life sciences, which are not primarily medical. The term 'bioethics' offers two advantages. Firstly, it suggests a much wider concern than simply rules of behaviour for a particular guild. Secondly, it connotes more broadly contemporary health care's focus on the 'bio-realm', for example, areas such as lifestyle, diet, stress management, physical and social environment, etc. The term 'bio-realm' suggests a much more inclusive universe of concerns than does 'medical realm'.

The explosion of knowledge in the life sciences created a proliferation of ethical problems that required special study. Increased capability (discovering foetal characteristics before birth, transplanting body organs, etc.) means that certain medical interventions that were hitherto impossible have become possible. The question is: ought we accept them? Increased knowledge, for example, the discovery of the impact of the use of certain spray cans on the ozone layer and of the effect of proximity to nuclear energy plants on prenatal development, raises questions about the value-system underlying this new knowledge. Bioethics offers a wider canvas to reflect on these and the many new issues confronting medicine, ethics and society today. For example, ethicists' and health-care professionals' new desire to consider moral principles governing institutions and societies has forced attention to questions of medical justice. Should we spend more on basic health care or on exotic life-saving devices such as artificial hearts?

Humankind has acquired unprecedented power to shape and reshape its biological and psychological nature. Bioethics attempts to ensure that this power is used to respect and protect human dignity. It addresses itself to the most urgent problems of humankind, such as water and air pollution, population explosion and the physiological and psychological effects of urban conglomeration.

The distinction between bioethics and medical ethics has a parallel in the distinction between 'health economics' and 'health-care economics'. Health-care economics is the study of the economics of the provision of health-care services. Health economics is the study of all aspects of life that affect health, e.g. pollution, road safety, etc. This broad concept is closely allied to 'health promotion' – the promotion of all government policies that improve health, including pollution control, etc.

Bioethics allows medicine to experience how humanity's existence is affected by its environment, and makes it necessary for the medical profession to assume responsibility for the world around it and to discern better what genuine therapy and human progress mean in a perspective of human dignity and freedom. Bioethics concerns itself with questions of vision, value and meaning. Bioethics considers the unfolding of life and its protection, health and healing, death and dying as all decisive focal points of social responsibility. Bioethics cannot be separated from the broader task of building up a healthy world.

The application of such principles as 'do no harm' and 'respect for the sanctity of life' are no longer clear. Other questions that arise include how ethical principles can conflict with each other, what specific rules of conduct should be, and whether those rules should be binding in every circumstance. All applications of general ethical principles to particular fields presuppose a co-operation between ethicists and experts in a particular area, because, although the bioethicist explicitly confronts the ethical question, this is possible only on the advice of the relevant expert. Thus, bioethics is an interdisciplinary enterprise, challenged to have the courage and integrity to take its place in the pluralistic market-place of the society it serves, recognising that in so doing it will have to run the risk of having its views rejected as well as respected by society.

The medical profession has extraordinary powers. These powers bring awesome responsibilities. On what basis does the ethicist claim to pass judgement on matters relating to medical care and the procedures of medical science? Ethics extends to the whole of life and so there can be no legitimate compartmentalisation of the ethical and medical spheres. The ethicist can also help the health-care professional to raise the right questions, e.g. is the criterion of what is good giving way to the criterion of what is useful? The good and the useful may coincide but they do not necessarily do so.

One quality that the ethicist lacks is omniscience. In medieval times a doctoral thesis was presented bearing the title, *Concerning everything that is known.* Such a notion is laughable today. While there have been great advances in our knowledge, the downside is that nobody is in a position to see the whole picture. In a sense bioethics is principally concerned with what health-care professionals ought to do when they are not sure what to do.

The Last Word

Medical ethics is sometimes perceived as being excessively individualistic. Perhaps what might help, even as an educational exercise, is that we introduce a new principle of community, beyond the four traditional principles we have considered. This might help us to grapple seriously with the tension between the claims of individuals and the claims of communities.

In health-care economics four questions predominate:
- How much money is to be spent on health care?
- How is this money to be allocated within the health services?
- What is it that this money can buy?
- How are decisions to be made?

The answers to the first two questions are ultimately political ones. The third question defines the options available. The fourth is a question that all of us have a stake in and should have an input in. The debate about the allocation of scarce resources in health care raises fundamental questions about the type of society we wish to live in.

The eighteenth-century theologian, Joseph Butler, pointed to the twin drives within all of us to self-love and benevolence, and claimed that ethics is not necessarily a matter of antagonism or inner struggle between these drives, but more a matter of achieving and maintaining the right balance between being ego-centred and ego-transcending. This offers a wonderful conceptual framework for a discussion on ethical dilemmas, but how is this balance to be achieved in practice?

Contemporary society correctly places great emphasis on the rights of the individual. However, a proliferation of institutions from the European Union to the World Council of Churches bear testimony to the interdependence of humankind and stress co-operation and group action. The last word on the topic goes to the British Prime Minister Tony Blair: 'In reality the Christian message is that the self is best realised through communion with others. The act of Holy Communion is symbolic of this message. It acknowledges that we do not grow up in total independence, but interdependently.'

A GLOBAL ETHIC:
A REFLECTION ON A TRIP TO PAKISTAN

The focus of the preceding chapters has been unashamedly on the medical profession in Ireland. However, mindful of the dangers of parochialism, it would be remiss of me in a book attempting to deal with contemporary ethical issues in medicine to exclude the wider international issues. My reflections in this area have been largely shaped by personal experience.

From the moment you enter the baggage area of Lahore Airport you are confronted by intense poverty. To see this on television is akin to watching *Ally McBeal* or *The Simpsons*. You say to yourself, this can not really happen. But when the stark reality is but feet away from you, it is frightening in the extreme.

The agonising tyranny of the plight of the majority struck me most forcefully on a visit to the slums only ten minutes from the paradisal world of the leafy suburbs, which are home to the wealthy élite. There the diet of mystically nourishing pap of half-formed truths that I had been fed about the advances in the lot of the poor retreated into the womb of delusion.

Pakistan is a highly stratified, paternalistic society, without even a notion of *noblesse oblige*. It seems that the lot of the poor is to live frugally on the crumbs from the wealthy élite's tables.

A Lullaby for Tasmin

All seem soaked in a heavy despondency as if some totally melancholy spirit brooded over the place. Flies feast on the sea of slurry, and the buzz of their relish produces a faint hum in the air. It might have been the Sahara desert rather than a *basti* (slum) in Lahore. Poverty is sucking the vitality out of it as a bee sucks honey out of a flower. The basti, foul-smelling and decrepit, is a monument to broken hearts and foiled aspirations, to innumerable tales of sadness and dawning shreds of hope. It is easy to imagine that the stinking stench would upset the stomach of a horse.

There are thousands like it throughout Pakistan, and every one tells the same story. Illness. Hunger. The death of hope. A person, it is held, can become accustomed to anything, but poverty for these people is a recurring nightmare. In the *basti*, as in most places, money, or more precisely the lack of it, makes all the difference. It is difficult not to succumb to a great sense of the desolation of life that sweeps all round like a tidal wave, drowning all in its blackness.

To get an insight into family life I am taken to a family home. The mother greets me, a total stranger, warmly like a long lost friend. There is grace and poise in her walk, though a coat of dirt films her shoes. Her eyes roam the one-room dwelling with a quick, intelligent sweep when we step inside. She hurries to the corner of the room, where a sick child lies tossing to and fro in the bed. Tasmin is now in the full grip of fever. She is two weeks old, a pale little thing with black eyes set in a small face. Her face is drenched in sweat and the blue towel near her head is quite wet. The baby's little hands jerk convulsively outside the tiny blanket. She looks pathetically small in the bed, a tiny martyr in the grip of illness. Instinctively the mother is terribly afraid.

She kneels beside the cradle. In the stillness, there is a noble humility about her kneeling figure. So still is she that she looks like a statue called out of darkness itself. As if transfixed, she stares at the little face, still deadly pale despite the thick coat of sweat. Suddenly Tasmin's eyes open wide and nothing has ever seemed so huge to me as those black jewels. They stare long at me as if sensing my concern. Almost in spite of myself I look deep down into their depths and I know that this child is suffering a great deal. The little, fragile hands open and close as if registering arrows of pain shooting through her frail body.

As if by magic the baby falls asleep again; an uneasy fitful sleep, marked by pained little whimperings that cut like swords of sorrow into the mother's heart. Occasionally, the little body twitches convulsively as if it is going to break into little pieces. Every time it convulses, the mother leans forward anxiously as if beseeching God to allow her to bear the stabs of pain that needle through the little creature. Although her eyes are closed, the baby is sweating profusely. From time to time her mother leans forward to wipe the baby's face and neck with the soft towel she has kept nearby. Her face is grey and fatigued, bearing the marks of incredible strain. A few days earlier she had felt the cold of death spread through every limb and bone in the baby's twin sister until she was very cold and stiff. It was only then that the torture had left her face and a soft peacefulness set on it like a child on a Christmas card. That night her mother's screams tore like knives into the heart of silence, ripping it relentlessly asunder. There was an animal-like quality to her wailing, powered by notes of horrifying, intense pain and desperation. Her screams fell like a sentence on the room.

Although the heat is stifling, not once does the mother's head nod towards sleep; not once does she lift her eyes from the baby's body. She smiles at me and in that moment the fellowship of the besieged is clearly established. Her patience seems infinite. Time does not matter, for her it does not exist. In her eyes the universe is centred in that child so small that she scarcely ruffled the blankets. She sits beside baby Tasmin, listening to her breathing, feeling her body twitch slightly as her restless mind fled through the corridors of her dreams. Occasionally she strokes her forehead. So delicately light is her touch, her fingers scarcely seem to fondle the baby's fingers. They are like frail fingers of gossamer brushing her tiny hands. Her vigil of love continues.

When the baby wakes up the mother takes her in her arms. To my horror she passes Tasmin to me. I have never been more petrified. I have often held a baby but never a creature like this. Her arms and legs are as thin as pencils and I pray I wouldn't break any of her bones. She weighs no more than a bar of chocolate. After a few minutes I gratefully return her to the hands that rock her cradle.

As I leave the 'house' I wonder will Tasmin survive the night.

Children of a Lesser God

It sounds like a macabre plot from a novel by Charles Dickens. However, the problem of child exploitation in Pakistan is fact not fiction. According to one estimate there are nine million child labourers in Pakistan, with poverty being the single most important factor contributing to this human tragedy. In the city of Lahore alone, it is calculated that half a million children are victims of slave labour. Parents with large families hate to send their children to work but the options before them are stark: starve at home or survive at work. On low wages a family cannot survive with just one wage earner. Where child labour is available in the market, employers simply substitute them for their adult labour since they can bully them into accepting low wages.

The biggest offender is the carpet industry. It is a labour-intensive industry and carpets are produced at a cheap price to be more competitive in the international market. Employers like children because they learn the designing lessons quicker than adults. A Swedish television documentary exposed shocking evidence of this bonded labour. According to the film there are twenty million bonded workers in the country in different industries, which include 50,000 children working in the carpet industry alone.

One interviewee, twelve-year-old Nadeem, told how he had started work at the age of four and was sold from owner to owner. He has frequently being beaten not only with a stick and panja (carpet fork) but his fingers were also cut by a knife. He was chained to the loom at which he worked and was forced to work up to twelve or thirteen hours daily. Two sisters, Shaheen and Naseem, from Lahore alleged that they were repeatedly molested from the age of eight by the carpet factory owner and his brothers where they were working. They alleged that the police refused to take any action against the carpet owner, who was an influential figure in the area.

Another interviewee was Khawaja Salahuddin Admad Sahaf, carpet exporter and former president of Lahore Chamber of Commerce and Industry. Initially he rejected the existence of child labour but later claimed that no country can produce carpets without child labour. A carpet factory owner said he has 100 looms, with about 400 children working on them. He claimed that it was good that children were used because they were obedient and hard working. An additional problem for children in the carpet industry is that they often fall prey to TB (a disease that is as prevalent in Pakistan today as it was in the pre-Noel Browne days in Ireland) and also defects in the legs.

Not surprisingly a Westerner gets a hostile reception when attempting to examine one of these factories but I did manage to snatch a glance inside the door of a factory in the city of Sargoda. The ghastly nightmare of these children was all too apparent. Two young girls were working frantically, one looked no more that five years of age, the other could be no more than seven. A man with what appeared to be a big stick hovered ominously in the background.

Outside, three Government jets, F-16s, costing a reputed twenty million dollars each, fly overhead, apparently on a military exercise. It is a real parable of the 'third world'. A huge portion of Pakistan's national wealth is sucked up by the army, though, as in many areas of Pakistani life, it is difficult to get a precise figure. It has been remarked that Otto Von Bismarck's observation about Prussia is equally applicable to Pakistan: 'While in other European nations the military works for the State, in Prussia the State was for the military'. There are also rumours about Pakistan's alleged escalating nuclear force.

Another major offender is workshops, where children endure inhuman treatment at the hands of their 'Ustads'. According to reports, these bosses regularly inflict corporal punishment. Children are chained, slapped, beaten with iron rods and are made go without food for days. Such children are 'owned' by their Ustads and considered sub-humans. Often they eat stale and left-out food, and sleep in parks, in parked buses, on footpaths or wherever they might get lodging for the night.

A third major area of abuse are restaurants, where hired boys are compelled to work from dawn to midnight and sometimes beyond. Their sleeping quarters may just be the store of the restaurants, on a dirty quilt laid out on the floor. Often they have rats and cockroaches as sleeping companions.

Pakistan has signed the Declaration on the Rights of the Child and passed laws like the Employment of Children Act 1991 and Bonded Labour Abolition Act 1992. The problem is not the product of inadequate laws but a failure to implement them. Child exploitation is a long way from the top of the political agenda in Pakistan.

That night I meet three emaciated ten-year-old girls – obviously exhausted from a twelve-hour day at the carpet factory. One of them is coughing alarmingly. How much longer can her health sustain this daily assault on her bodily integrity?

What's Love Got to Do With It?

A sea of suffering. A typical tourist, I have made my way to the markets, but like all Westerners I am surrounded by a seemingly unending mass of beggars. Each has some form of disability. When the storm abates I casually ask if there is any reason why there are so many disabled people in Pakistan and am informed that it has a lot to do with the attitude to marriage.

Marriage practices in Asia differ dramatically from those of the Western world. For example, in May 1994 several hundred children aged under seven were married in the northern Indian State of Rajasthan in defiance of a law banning child marriage. Hundreds of boys and girls walked in traditional style around the fire to become husband and wife. The marriages in the State were performed on the day of a local Hindu festival despite a campaign by the authorities to stop this age-old practice. The authorities' efforts to clamp down on this practice have proved unsuccessful because many children, belonging to poor families, are married clandestinely without any marriage processions or fanfare. The custom dates back centuries to the time when the Moguls from central Asia conquered much of India. The Muslim invaders pillaged and plundered but would not touch a girl if she was married. Today, the custom is still considered as a way of protecting a girl's purity. But the main impetus is economic. Poor families often want to be free of their children and having many weddings at the same time cuts down on the costs.

In Pakistan the problem is the polar opposite. Families go all out to make their offspring's wedding a grand affair and frequently acquire enormous debts in the process – which cripple them financially for years. Another problem is that many families, prompted by a desire to keep their money within the family, favour intermarriage. As might be expected, this causes many of the children born out of these unions to be severely disabled.

As beggars, loneliness is their roll call. There is nothing in life but to endure and carry on. Each new day breaks on the world with its own pain and misery. It is like living life in a revolving door. They are infected by this emotional deprivation. Only when they get a tiny offering from a stranger does, for a brief moment, the chasm between their dreams and reality end.

Most of those with a mental illness are locked up and hidden away. The process of institutionalisation is itself a form of psychological internment, a malignant force that reduces people to human vegetables, incapable of independent thought. The primary objective is docility, the inmates are no longer a 'menace' to society. Like condemned prisoners serving out their sentences they are compelled to bathe communally, just another humiliation in a long catalogue of degradation. The erosion of personal dignity and privacy, the dead emotions and listless eyes are unavoidable side-effects to keep the system flowing smoothly. Nobody seems to question or even notice the perversion in the situation where the system becomes more important than the people it is designed to serve.

The Village

It is a typical farming village. Ninety per cent of the population of Pakistan are involved in agriculture, largely without modern farm equipment. The grain crops are cut with a hook and collected by hand. The threshing is carried out by hand, as is the winnowing. The common beast of burden is the buffalo, seen drawing the cart filled with hay, harvest or sugar cane. Most of the land is owned by a minority of landlords, so the majority of people are employed as farm labourers without any of the rights of even tenant farmers. Because of illiteracy and poverty, they are indeed the voiceless people. Ninety-five per cent of women and 84 per cent of men are illiterate in Pakistan; the result of this is plain to be seen in society – with a primitive lifestyle, poverty, sickness and suffering.

The average lifespan for ordinary people is only fifty because there is no village sanitation – people have to go into the fields, with the resultant effect of vermin and disease. No one other than the extremely affluent has the luxury of taps in their houses. The remainder have to make do with the village wells. In Pakistan there is no social welfare, so the family and extended family are essential as breadwinners to each other. For Christians there are additional problems. They are disadvantaged in seeking work and having limited promotional possibilities, e.g. in hospitals Christians are given only the lowly tasks and cannot expect advancement.

Infections and diseases prevalent in Pakistan include cholera and typhoid. There is much malnutrition and chest infection and women die of child-bearing related disease. The problems are exacerbated because the patients tend to go to hospitals as a last resort, having spent all their money doing the rounds of the 'pirs', i.e. the local healing men who do traditional healing and the quacks and unqualified medics who 'advise' the sick.

Their quality of life leaves much to be desired, with their average mud-brick house being of two rooms only, with a flat roof for sleeping on top. Their family size is on average six surviving children, with an accompanying high mortality rate.

Life is difficult for a Muslim woman if she is divorced, which the husband can do by merely saying three times: 'I divorce you'. She then has to go back to her own family for survival or, if they are dead, hopefully another family will take her in. Muslim men can have two or three wives simultaneously.

With a population of 130 million people, the highest illiteracy rate in the world, and the majority of the people living in rural areas, development from grass roots level will be a slow process. Over 4 per cent suffer from severe malnutrition and 72 per cent of all children's deaths occur in those under two years of age during the weaning period. Other common causes of death in children are diarrhoea, tetanus, measles, diphtheria and respiratory infections, including TB. Most of these diseases are preventable.

Looking around the village with its appalling sanitation and the black clouds of feasting flies, it is a health-care professional's worst nightmare. In this sea of suffering my despair sinks to new depths.

To look behind the faces of the people is to discover the harshest realities of existence. It is impossible to visit Pakistan and not feel anger. Anyone who knows the reality of life in the developing world cannot but strive for a new world order.

More positively, it is noteworthy in this context that the World Health Organisation's strategy of 'Health for All' puts heavy emphasis on primary health care. These strategies have played an invaluable role in the developing world in pursuing practical policies in such fundamental areas as the provision of clean water, food, education, housing, sanitation, adequate income, hygiene, and preventive medicine. These policies have led to both increased life expectancy and a better quality of life for millions of people. Although the WHO correctly states the ideal, it deals with the reality. Such an approach is advocated in the WHO's criteria:

> If health for all is to be reached . . . two basic issues must be tackled. The first is to reduce health inequalities among countries and among groups within countries. All the people of the Region should be assured an equal opportunity to develop, maintain and use their health. Particular efforts should therefore be made to provide for those countries, groups and individuals who lack it most. The second issue is to strengthen health, as much as to reduce disease and its consequences.

According to the WHO, 'Health for All' has four dimensions as regards health outcomes, involving action to:

- *ensure equity in health*, by reducing the present gap in health status between countries and groups within countries;
- *add life to years,* by ensuring the full development and use of people's integral or residual physical and mental capacity to derive full benefit from and to cope with life in a healthy way;
- *add health to life,* by reducing disease and disability;
- *add years to life,* by reducing premature deaths, and thereby increasing life expectancy.

A Global Ethic
Millions of people in Pakistan in particular and hundreds of millions of people in the developing world in general have poor health. It is not a clinical problem, an education problem, a political problem, a social problem, an economic problem, or a personnel problem, but a

combination of all of the above. The solution to these problems will demand action on all of these levels. Following her trip to famine-struck Somalia in 1992, the then President Mary Robinson frequently spoke of the need for a 'global ethic'. If the problems of health care for the starving millions in the developing world are to be adequately addressed, they must be considered in the wider context of: the threat to economic justice and human dignity from national security states, militaristic oligarchies and consumerist cultures; the questions of a just and sustainable international development; global trade arrangements; the influence of multinational corporations and regional economic communities; the conflicting trends of globalisation and tribalisation; the replacement of the East-West polarity of the Cold War with increasing North-South tensions over trade, debt, development and ecology; regional crises around food and energy supplies; and the presence of massive refugee populations.

The intolerable condition of many women around the world has become obvious to all. In Pakistan, for example, to speak of the 'option for the poor' is to speak of the option for women. The economic, political and cultural disadvantages suffered by women are a violation of justice and a serious threat to their lives. For all the talk of women's liberation, many women have not significantly improved their lot or achieved legal, economic or cultural parity. A major challenge today is to assess critically how we might most effectively confront the local, national and global systems oppressing and alienating women and men.

Karl Marx wrote: 'Philosophers have only interpreted the world. The point, however, is to change it'. As the Pakistani experience suggests, the challenge facing health-care professionals is enormous. For too long the international community has stood idly by. No one has seemed willing or able to take on the powerful vested interests that condemn so many millions of people to poverty and poor health. A new world order built on a global ethic is urgently required. The time for action is now. At stake is the very future of humankind.

Conclusion

WHERE DO WE GO FROM HERE?

President John F. Kennedy shortly after his election claimed that the key issue of the modern times is the management of industrial society – a problem of ways and means, not of ideology: 'The fact of the matter is that most of the problems, or at least many of them, that we now face are technical problems, are administrative problems [necessitating] . . . very sophisticated judgments which do not lend themselves to the great sort of "passionate movements" which have stirred this country so often in the past'. His analysis has proven to be seriously defective insofar as philosophical questions continue to be crucially important in finding answers to the value-related issues that have emerged with technological progress.

The noted writer on the genetics revolution, Bryan Appleyard, has spoken about the dangers of a 'moral free market'. He claims further, 'If the only value is that everybody makes up their own mind about everything, then, plainly, there is no value. There is only the persuasive power of the dominant forces of the age. We shall have become shrunken, more spiritually impoverished entities, but, perhaps luckily, we shall be too stupid to be aware of that fact.'

The problems today in teasing out the respective values of ethical dilemmas are compounded by the fact that much moral philosophy in our pluralist culture is apparently characterised by a fog of confusion. The leading American philosopher Alasdair MacIntyre has illustrated this problem by surveying a number of areas of contemporary debate – just war and anti-war theories in a nuclear age, the competing demands of pro- and anti-abortionists, and the competing demands of libertarians and those holding a strong theory of social justice. He claims:

> The most striking feature of contemporary moral utterance is that so much of it is used to express disagreements; and the most

striking feature of the debates in which these disagreements are
expressed is their interminable character. I do not mean by this
just that such debates go on and on and on – although they do
– but also that they apparently can find no terminus. There
seems to be no rational way of securing moral agreement in our
culture.[1]

As the old tree of established structures is dying it is not easy to
discern how to graft anew to the future vine. At the moment Ireland
is at an in-between time in its history, caught between a rich tradition
and an as yet unformed new direction. To misquote Aristotle, we can
only expect the precision and degree of certainty appropriate to the
subject matter. Sometimes the answers cannot be as neat and tidy as
we might like.

The fact that ethical principles are in the main *prima facie* ones
means that they cannot be applied woodenly. Discernment in
particular cases will always be required. The certainty that many crave
in moral issues is seldom to be had. The only thing we can be certain
of is uncertainty.

In the light of the profound societal and technological changes in
the post-World War Two period, a shared ethical system can no longer
be presumed. In such circumstances, the need shifts from a simple
consideration of etiquette to a more comprehensive approach to the
ethics of health care. Much of the current confusion in medical ethics
stems from the failure of the medical profession to address the
problem of a lack of conceptual framework in which the new
controversial issues in medicine can be adequately discussed.

The ethics of the health-care professions has evolved over many
years and reflects professional and societal changes. The current
understanding offers many helpful expressions of medicine's
professional obligations, but needs to be grounded in a more
comprehensive conceptual framework for an ethics of health care.

Historically, medical ethics has always lagged behind developments
in medical technology. Since its inception, medical ethics has been a
reactive discipline. To serve society adequately it must in the future
take more of a leadership role – anticipating questions that are likely

to arise. It does not take a crystal ball to know that the coming years will bring critical ethical questions.

A Parable For Our Time

In George Eliot's *Daniel Deronda,* Gwendolen Harleth married the revolting Grandcourt in order to provide money for her family. She hoped she would dominate him with the strength of her personality, but when she was unsuccessful she came to hate him. One day she was with him sailing in a small boat and was harbouring murderous thoughts against him when he was swept overboard, and though she tried to save him, he was drowned. He died while she was wishing death on him, so she felt that she was in a sense an accomplice to murder. She carries a deep sense of guilt around with her and feels she can never be forgiven.

In the turmoil she approached her friend Deronda and shared her feelings of guilt: 'I did kill him in my thoughts. . . . It can never be altered'. Deronda listened patiently and displayed great insight into the human condition:

> He held it likely that Gwendolen's remorse aggravated her inward guilt. . . . But her remorse was the precious sign of a recoverable nature. . . . Deronda could not utter one word to diminish that sacred aversion to her worst self – that thorn-pressure which must come with the crowning of the sorrowful Better suffering because of the Worse. All this mingled thought and feeling kept him silent: speech was too momentous to be ventured on rashly. There were no words of comfort that did not carry some sacrilege. If he had opened his lips to speak, he could only have echoed, 'It can never be altered – it remains unaltered, to alter other things'.

Deronda handles the situation exceptionally well. He does not attempt to tell her she is wrong to condemn herself; he does not seek to take her pain away from her; he does not try to replace her flood of grief and accusation with soothing clichés of comfort. It would not be in Gwendolen's interests not to take seriously the wrong she feels she has been guilty of. However, he is aware that in the hour of darkness she has come, for the first time, to that point of self-knowledge when the 'worst' side of her nature has been absorbed and that she will not grow unless she is allowed to have the pain of knowledge.

While she did not cause her husband's death, it was accompanied by her own murderous thoughts. Hers is, to use the traditional term, a sin of the heart. Neither event can be undone: her husband will remain dead, and she cannot change what she felt towards him, but from Deronda's perspective, these terrible events can alter other things, i.e. how she lives the rest of her life. Deronda initiates the process of healing by taking seriously the struggle within Gwendolen – who for the first time is confronted with the truth of her nature.

In this way the events of the past can alter the future since something new has been introduced into Gwendolen's experience. The tyranny of the past can be broken; the sin of the past can be healed in the future – not by minimising the seriousness of the past, but by putting the past in the perspective of a different future.

The medical profession cannot undo the damage or pain it has caused to Charlotte Yates or Bernard Smullen. What it can do is to make the changes that will ensure patients will never suffer in this way again.

The scandals we have considered and the personal testimonies we have examined underline the need for radical surgery in the medical profession, in the practice of medicine and in the health-care system, and not simply band-aid solutions. Rather than waiting for the problems to arise and resorting to crisis management it would be more constructive to have adequate safeguards in place to ensure that people's integrity will not be trampled on in the future. As any doctor will tell you, prevention is better than cure.

Note

1. Alasdair MacIntyre, *After Virtue* (Duckworth, 1981), p. 6.

SELECT BIBLIOGRAPHY

Beauchamp, Tom. *Philosophical Ethics.* New York: Harper & Row, 1969.

Costello, Declan. 'The Terminally Ill: The Law's Concerns'. *Doctrine and Life,* Vol. 38, (Feb 1988), pp. 69-78.

Duncan, A. S., et al, eds. *A New Dictionary of Medical Ethics.* London: DLT, 1981.

Fuchs, Josef. *Christian Morality: The Word Becomes Flesh.* Washington DC: Georgetown University Press, 1987.

Garwood-Gowers, Austen. *Living Donor Organ Transplantation: Key Legal and Ethical Issues.* Dartmouth: Ashgate Publishing, 1999.

Gillon, Raanan, ed. *Principles of Health Care Ethics.* London, 1994.

Häring, Bernard. *Medical Ethics.* Slough: St Paul, 1991.

Irish Catholic Bishops' Conference. *Prosperity with a Purpose.* Dublin: Veritas, 1999.

Jones, D. Gareth. *Speaking for the Dead: Cadavers in Biology and Medicine.* Dartmouth: Ashgate Publishing, 1999.

Kearon, Kenneth. *Medical Ethics: An Introduction.* Dublin: Columba Press, 1995.

McCormick, Richard. *The Critical Calling.* Milwaukee: Marquette University Press, 1989.

Mahoney, John. *Bioethics and Belief.* London: Sheed & Ward, 1984.

Poole, Joyce. *The Cross of Unknowing: Dilemmas of a Catholic Doctor.* London: Sheed & Ward, 1989.

Ramsey, Paul. *The Patient as Person.* New Haven: Yale University Press, 1978.

Rawls, John. *A Theory of Justice.* Cambridge, Mass: Harvard University Press, 1971.

Reich, W. T. *Encylopedia of Bioethics.* London: Collier Macmillan, 1983.

Reidy, Maurice, ed. *Ethical Issues in Reproductive Medicine.* Dublin: Gill and Macmillan, 1982.

Scally, John. *Whose Death is It Anyway? Euthanasia and the Right to Die.* Dublin: Basement Press, 1995

Scally, John, ed. *Ethics in Crisis?* Dublin: Veritas, 1997.

Scally, John. *After the Brave New World?* Dublin: Veritas, 1998.

Sigerist, Henry E. *A History of Medicine.* New York: Oxford University Press, 1972.

Smith, David. *Life and Morality.* Dublin: Gill and Macmillan, 1995.

Shannon, T. A., ed. *Bioethics.* New York: Paulist Press, 1993.

Tomkin, David and Hanafin, Patrick. *Irish Medical Law.* Dublin: The Round Hall Press, 1995.

World Council of Churches. *Biotechnology: Its Challenges to the Churches and the World,* 1989.